CAREERS
F O R
CLASS CLOWNS
& Other
Engaging Types

VGM Careers for You Series

CAREERS
FOR
CLASS
CLOWNS
& Other
Engaging Types

Jan Goldberg

VGM Career Horizons
NTC/Contemporary Publishing Group

0359037b

Library of Congress Cataloging-in-Publication Data

Goldberg, Jan.
    Careers for class clowns & other engaging types / Jan Goldberg.
       p.   cm. — (Careers for you series)
      ISBN 0-8442-4607-7 (cloth). — ISBN 0-8442-4622-0 (pbk.)
      1. Performing arts—Vocational guidance. 2. Juggling—Vocational
guidance. 3. Clowning—Vocational guidance. 4. Magicians—
Vocational guidance.   I. Title. II. Series.
   PN1580.G568   1998
   791'.023—dc21   98–29473
                                            CIP

Published by VGM Career Horizons
A division of NTC/Contemporary Publishing Group, Inc.
4255 West Touhy Avenue, Lincolnwood (Chicago), Illinois 60646-1975 U.S.A.
Copyright © 1999 by NTC/Contemporary Publishing Group, Inc.
Printed in the United States of America
International Standard Book Number: 0-8442-4607-7 (cloth)
                                    0-8442-4622-0 (paper)

18   17   16   15   14   13   12   11   10   9   8   7   6   5   4   3   2   1

This book is dedicated to the
memory of my beloved parents,
Sam and Sylvia Lefkovitz,
and to a dear aunt,
Estelle Lefko.

Contents

Acknowledgments ix

CHAPTER ONE
An Introduction to Clowning Around 1

CHAPTER TWO
Here Come the Clowns! 7

CHAPTER THREE
Comedians 35

CHAPTER FOUR
Jugglers and More 47

CHAPTER FIVE
Magicians 71

CHAPTER SIX
Performers 79

Name Quiz Answers 119

About the Author 121

Acknowledgments

*T*he author gratefully acknowledges:

- The numerous professionals who graciously agreed to be profiled in this book

- My dear husband Larry for his inspiration and vision

- My children, Deborah, Bruce, and Sherri, for their encouragement and love

- Family and close friends—Adrienne, Marty, Mindi, Cary, Michele, Paul, Michele, Alison, Steve, Marci, Steven, Brian, Jesse, Bertha, Uncle Bernard, and Aunt Helen for their faith and support

- Diana Catlin, for her insights and input

- Betsy Lancefield, editor at VGM, for making all projects rewarding and enjoyable

CHAPTER ONE

An Introduction to Clowning Around

"A well-developed sense of humor is the pole that adds balance to your steps as you walk the tightrope of life." WILLIAM A. WARD

D o you love attention—perhaps even crave it? Do people think you are funny? Do you like to think of yourself as entertaining? And do others agree? Are you happy when all eyes are on you? Has anyone ever referred to you as the class clown?

Class Clowns

Class clowns will use a myriad of devices, all designed to do one thing—make themselves the focus of attention. Those who actually engaged in this behavior in the schoolroom might have incurred the teacher's wrath at times, but were usually liked by classmates. In a way, they were often admired by them.

In the "real world," the class clown spirit can serve as a positive force for those individuals who thrive on being at the center of attention in their career of choice. Are you a class clown? Take the following quiz—and you'll find out!

The Class Clown Quiz

1. Do you enjoy being the center of attention?

2. Do you purposely do things that draw attention to you?

3. Are you most comfortable when you stand out from others?

4. Is ordinary not good enough for you?

5. Do you avoid being one of many?

6. Do you like to do your own thing?

7. Do you prefer to lead rather than follow?

8. Do you have a facility for entertaining others?

9. Are you gregarious?

10. Are you an extrovert?

11. Do you like to entertain?

12. Do you like to make others laugh?

13. Are you creative?

14. Can you memorize things easily?

15. Are you funny?

16. Are you unafraid of being in front of a group?

17. Do you enjoy performing?

18. Do you enjoy applause?

19. Do you like to travel?

20. Do you mind working nights and weekends?

21. Are you uncomfortable having a career that is unpredictable?

22. Do you have a pleasing personality?

23. Are you adept at selling yourself?

24. Do you like being your own boss?

25. Do you really enjoy being with people?

If you've answered yes to many of these questions, then read on. This book focuses on a number of careers that are perfect for those who possess these qualities or tendencies.

Be a Clown!

The spirit of clowning has existed for thousands and thousands of years in civilizations all over the world. Individuals who have adopted clowning and other entertainment careers have made important contributions to society. These careers provide outlets for all of us. Entertainment allows people relief from common stresses and allows them to reenergize their efforts in their fields of choice and their daily lives.

A Short History of Clowning

Throughout history, most cultures have recorded the presence of clowns. Cortez found them when he conquered the Aztec nation in 1520 A.D. To a great degree, they were similar to the clowns that existed in Europe at that time.

Some types of clown characters were a part of most Native American tribes. They often played an important social and religious role in the society at the time. Some were believed to be capable of curing some diseases.

Some of the earliest ancestors of the clown were a part of ancient Greece. These comics were bald and padded to appear larger than normal. They were usually a part of farces and mime and they parodied the actions of the more serious characters. A similar character was also a part of Roman mime. This clown wore a pointed hat and colorful robe and was the target for all tricks and abuse of other characters in the production.

Jesters

Remember Court Jesters? Throughout the Middle Ages and in the early years of the Renaissance, jesters (or fools, as they were also called) perpetuated the art of clowning in the palaces of kings and well-known nobles. Jesters played a particularly important role in the social culture of Medieval Europe by serving as "safety valves" or a "social conscience." As they were the only ones allowed to speak out against the rulers' ideas, jesters were often catalysts for social change. Often they were able to wield considerable power through their wit and humor.

It was also during this time that colorful costumes associated with today's clowns had their origins. Jesters adopted a standard uniform of bright green and saffron colored coats, hose, and a hooded cap topped by tiny bells designed to tinkle whenever the wearer moved.

Historic Clowns

Although many clowns entertained at court, the vast majority were street performers. They were adept at a variety of skills, as is often the case with clowns today. They engaged in magic, contortion, juggling, acrobatics, storytelling, puppetry, tightrope walking, working with trained animals, ballad singing, clever dialogue, or any combination of the above.

"Zany," "jester," "fool," "minstrel," and "mime" are but a few of the historical synonyms for "clown." The English equivalent used today did not appear until the sixteenth century. "Clown" originally meant "clod" and was often used to denote a clumsy country bumpkin. These rustics were considered very funny, and comedic actors soon imitated their ways.

Among the first professional stage clowns were the famous William Keme and Robert Armin, both of whom were connected with Shakespeare's company. Through English traveling actors of the seventeenth century, Germany was introduced to stage clowns. One popular character is Pickelherring. He and his friends wore clown costumes that remain similar today—giant ruffs around their necks, hats, and oversized shoes.

At the same time, the spirit of improvisation reached new heights in Italy in the form of street theater. This gave birth to a roster of comedic characters that may still be seen today. These include Harlequin, with his popular patchwork costume, and Pierrot, one of the first clowns known to use whiteface.

The first real circus clown was Joseph Grimaldi, who first appeared in England in 1805. Grimaldi's clown called "Joey" specialized in the classic physical tricks, tumbling, and slapstick beatings. (Since then, clowns are often called "Joeys.") In the 1860s a low-comedy comic with a big nose, baggy clothes, large shoes, and untidy manners appeared under the name of Auguste. He worked with a clown in whiteface and always spoiled the latter's trick by appearing at the wrong time to mess things up.

Grock (Adrien Wettach), a famous pantomimist in whiteface, evoked laughter in his continual struggle with inanimate objects. Chairs collapsed beneath him. When a stool was too far from a piano, he shoved the piano to the stool. His elaborate melancholy resembled that of Emmett Kelly, the American vagabond clown.

The Big Top

By the end of the nineteenth century, the smaller tents of the one-ring show had given way to the "big top" and the circus enjoyed a golden age. As the large new three-ring format evolved, clowns were presented with their greatest challenge yet. Spectacular movement, bright costumes, oversized props, loud explosives, and flamboyant makeup became essential ingredients in the clown's new formula for laughs. By 1907 when the Ringling brothers purchased another popular circus, Barnum and Bailey, the profession of clowning had reached one of its highest peaks.

To preserve the rapidly dwindling profession, Irvin Feld founded Ringling Brothers and Barnum and Bailey Clown College in 1968, providing the first formal training ground for clowns. Since then, the college has had more than a thousand aspiring clowns pass through its doors, rejuvenating the whole career.

Clown College offers a varied and imaginative curriculum that reflects the skills and traditions of this ancient and international art. Always, an impressive faculty roster and star studded list of alumni have been among those affiliated with the college.

After teaching the basics in their Clown College for thirty years, Ringling Brothers and Barnum and Bailey Circus decided to stop offering the eight-week introductory classes. Instead, clowns already in the business can attend "Masters of Comedy" workshops. Kenneth Feld, chairman and chief executive of Feld Entertainment, which runs Ringing Brothers, is quoted as saying, "They know in eight weeks you can only learn so much. Then you go on the road and that becomes your graduate school. This will be like a master's class in clowning."

Clown College was the brainchild of Feld's late father, Irvin. "This is pretty exciting and new," says Feld, "but that doesn't mean that in a few years, we won't go back to what we had before."

What's in a Name?

When you become famous—whether as a circus clown, nightclub comedian, or performing artist—you might want to change your name and take on a "stage name" as so many other entertainers have done before you. Interspersed within the book are the birth names of some well-known comic entertainers. Look for them as you read the book. (Their more well-known stage names can be found at the end of the book.) Perhaps, someday, your name will also be listed among these notable entertainers!

Here's your first birth name challenge:
Jerome Silberman

CHAPTER TWO

Here Come the Clowns!

"Laughter can be more satisfying than honor, more precious than money, more heart-cleansing than prayer." HARRIET ROCHLIN

Clowning Around

Clowns divert and entertain audiences by performing comical routines, often while wearing unusual makeup and costumes. Actually, they are actors and comedians whose job is to make people laugh and have a good time. Often they wear outlandish costumes, paint their faces, and use a variety of performance skills to entertain audiences. To accomplish this, they may juggle, dance, walk on stilts, perform magic tricks, work creatively with balloons, make use of body antics, and a host of other skills.

Some clowns perform in large groups as they do in a circus. Circus clowns often perform routines while the rings are being prepared for other acts. They might sing songs, tell jokes, or do acrobatic stunts. Some of the routines they perform are written specifically for them (or they write them themselves). Others are well-known comedy routines.

Clowns must have a good sense of timing and balance and must be able to adjust their performances to the audience. They must have a good sense of humor, enjoy working and interacting with people, and have the ability to shift gears and adapt quickly to an audience.

Clowns come from all walks of life. But one thing they all have in common is that they are creative people who love to entertain. In "becoming" clowns, they often develop their own persona and their own acts or routines, which are a reflection of their personality or a personality they wish to portray.

How do you develop a clown character? Three key elements are 1) overall appearance, including costume, 2) makeup, and 3) personality. In order to correctly project their personas, the respective clown characters must wear appropriate costumes and makeup.

Types of Clowns

There are three basic types of clowns. Which appeals to you most?

Whiteface

Usually the white-faced clown is the "straight" clown in skits. He or she is easily identified by the makeup, which has a base of white grease paint. The "straight" clown is the one who acts very serious but who ends up being the brunt of the skit or the punch line. The costumes of white-faced clowns are usually more formal than other clowns. This means that the colors tend to match and the costume flows together. Other clown types tend to wear more gaudy or mismatched colors.

Makeup of the white-faced clown is typically simple and will highlight natural features (eyes, lips, cheeks) already present on the face. Variations of a white-faced clown are unlimited. There are no specific guidelines except the basic white base.

Auguste Clown

The silly clown in skits is usually the Auguste clown. Makeup for these clowns is a bright flesh-tone base. Auguste clowns will usually appear to be unaware of what's going on in the skit, but somehow manage to escape being the brunt of everything (called the "blow off"). Costumes of Auguste clowns tend to be gaudy, mismatched, and very bright. Primary colors are most popular and the clothing is usually oversized.

The makeup is usually bright and exaggerates the natural features already present in the face (large nose, large mouth, etc.). Again there are millions of variations and all clowns adapt their own special features, which become their trademarks.

Character Clown

The character clown is just what you would suspect—a character who is exaggerated into a clown. The most popular example of this is the Hobo or Tramp clown. This clown is usually seen with tattered clothes including a worn hat, a red nose, makeup that suggests a week's worth of a beard, and other exaggerated features.

Character clowns can be from almost any walk of life. Some of the other more well-known examples are police officers, women, or babies.

Where the Clowns Are!

Clowns work in a variety of places—circuses, movies, on television, in fairs, musical plays, or fairgrounds or amusement parks. Many clowns work for commercial employers—Ronald McDonald, for instance, who is almost synonymous for McDonald's franchises. Some clowns work at rodeos. Their job is to distract the bull when a cowboy falls off a horse. This is serious work because slapping the bull in the face is a risky business.

Other clowns are self-employed and may entertain at parties, birthday celebrations, school shows, senior citizen events, country or state parks, trade shows, or conventions. They may work at automobile shows or shopping malls. Their job is to attract the attention of passersby and direct their attention to the event. Many clowns work an established circuit to make a living.

Shrine Clowns

Some clowns are Shrine Clowns and belong to the International Shrine Clown Association. These clowns work to cheer up children who are in Shrine hospitals and work in a variety of other ways to raise money for Shrine causes. As members, they receive newsletters and may attend conferences. Members report that they reap great personal rewards for engaging in the International Shrine Clown Association's efforts.

The Circus Is in Town

There are about thirty large circuses and a hundred or so smaller traveling shows that entertain in shopping malls, at state and country fairs, and in similar locations.

Circus people travel. They may set up their show in fifty or sixty towns between April and October (Ringling Brothers and Barnum and Bailey Circus tours from January through November). The stops in one place may last only a day, two or three days, or as long as five weeks. Winter quarters are often in Florida and California but might be in Texas, Missouri, Oklahoma, New Jersey, or another place.

At one time, circuses traveled by train and used horse-drawn wagons to parade through towns and set up the big top. Then truck shows began to travel the circuit. Today, compact truck and bus convoys carry equipment, performers, and animals. Performers may travel in their own air-conditioned motor homes. Many circus people stay at motels or hotels when they perform in one place for several days. At every town, a circus staff member picks up and distributes personal mail to the performers.

Trains are still in use, however. Ringling Brothers and Barnum and Bailey Circus has two fifty-plus-car trains. They carry all the equipment and animals and have staterooms for performers.

A cook tent, which may be part of the circus, serves meals throughout the tour. A flag raised above the cook tent indicates that the meal is ready. Ringling Brothers has a dining car on the train and dining accommodations at the arena for the performers.

Generally, large circuses now perform indoors in stadiums, arenas, and large halls. Many small ones, however, still play under canvas tents. No two places are the same. Each stop presents special restrictions. The circus must obey local safety and health laws. Many towns insist on inspections and permits before they let the circus perform. While the arena may be large and comfortable in one city, the next city's circus site may be smaller or more difficult to perform in.

Circus performers on the road have few free hours. Although their acts take only a short time, they give two shows a day, and sometimes three, afternoons and evenings, Sundays and holidays. They also practice or rehearse between shows. A flawless performance and perfect timing come only after years of hard work and practice. They take care of costumes, set up and take down equipment, put on makeup, do other tasks related to their performance, and may have other assigned tasks. Their time is seldom their own.

Roll in the Clowns

Clowns, with their comic antics, relieve the tension of the dangerous acts. Many clowns are physical performers. They may ride horseback or do tightwire acts. Some are jugglers, acrobats, or musicians.

When the ring conductor blows the whistle to signal the start of a show, all entertainers and animals join the opening parade around the arena track. A circus performance consists of three to four dozen acts. The band conductor and musicians play the music for each act. All acts are timed, and acts going on in all three rings finish at the same time.

The Road to Clowning

Like other actors, clowns benefit from a solid education. A high school diploma is not required by most circuses, but a diploma and a college education certainly help a clown's job prospects. Employers in the motion picture and television industry also prefer to hire performers who have diplomas.

Many high schools have drama or dance classes for students. Shows are put on regularly by high school and community centers. Experience acting or performing in plays is very important. Dance academies, schools for dramatic arts, and colleges and universities offer classes in pantomime and dance. Clowns need to move well and be able to use their bodies to communicate. Training in magic, juggling, acrobats, clown makeup, costuming, choreography, and the history of clowning is also important.

Clowns also need to learn to project their voices. Debate or public speaking clubs or classes can help to develop this.

As mentioned in Chapter 1, Ringling Brothers and Barnum and Bailey Circus has a clown college. The tuition is free, but those who are accepted must pay room and board, a materials fee, and provide their own transportation and spending money. Applicants must be under twenty-five years of age.

A small number of students from the many applications are chosen to participate in the annual ten-week course in Sarasota, Florida. There are usually about forty to sixty spots to fill. From this elite group, a select few will tour with Ringling Brothers and Barnum and Bailey. No prior experience is necessary. They accept people from all walks of life—from professional clowns to recent high school graduates to former rocket scientists!

Every trip, fall, and stumble that a clown takes on the arena floor has been intricately choreographed long beforehand and is the result of months, even years, of intensive training. While at Clown College, each student undergoes rigorous gymnastic instruction, learning to perform somersaults, back flips, and tumbling runs. They even learn to launch themselves over a specialized vaulting horse in any number of comedic positions. In addition, students have an opportunity to practice comic acrobatic falls and safety techniques for performing slapstick comedy. In fact, in every stunt the clowns attempt, safety is the watchword. Protective padding is worn, tumbling mats are strategically placed to break a fall and provide a soft "landing," and students progress according to their individual levels of ability. So the next time you see a bumbling, stumbling clown tumbling into a heap, remember you're watching a trained professional in action!

Here's a sample ad for a clown:

Requirements

You must be:

- funny

- a high school graduate (or hold a GED certificate)

- funny

- able to work legally in the USA

- funny

- available to tour for the next year if selected to join the Greatest Show On Earth

- and FUNNY!

Compensation and Outlook for Clowns

Although there are no set salaries for clowns, the following represents average salaries. Remember, however, that clowns usually do not receive paid vacations or retirement benefits.

- Birthday parties—$50 to $150 for a thirty- to ninety-minute show

- Festivals or rodeos—$100 to $200 per engagement

- Circus clown—$200 to $500 weekly plus room and board

- Outside show—$50 to $4000 depending on skills and customer

- TV/film—$300 to $1000 average weekly income during peak season

The outlook for people who want to work as clowns is not very promising. There is a tremendous amount of competition, and the field is overcrowded, as it is in other segments of the entertainment industry. Wages may be controlled by unions. Like most performing artists, most clowns are not permanently employed and must repeatedly audition for positions. Clowns often don't receive the proper recognition for their work.

Tips for Getting into Clowning

One way to get into a circus is to find one and ask the manager for any work available. Often the circus needs workers to sell tickets and refreshments, or to water and exercise the animals. Some performers have a booking agent or personal manager. Others put ads in trade magazines. Performers with a good act might ask the directors or managers of state and country fairs, television shows, and nightclubs for an audition. Performers not yet established may find work at carnivals, amusement parks, ocean piers, rodeos, ice and water shows, and other places that draw spectators.

Words from the Pros

Introducing Gumdrop the Clown

Melo Dee Pisha of Peoria, Illinois, perhaps better known as Gumdrop the Clown, attended some traditional college and then went on to a succession of clown sites, including Clown Camp at the University of Wisconsin, Mooseburger University at the University of Minnesota, and clown conventions and workshops in the United States and England.

She also sought instruction as an actor–director and trained others in theater and clown skills in local schools and park districts. She recently directed a Peoria production of *Charlie and the Chocolate Factory*. Her challenges included a cast of fifty children, ages eight through eighteen.

"Everything started about fourteen years ago," she says. "I answered an ad in the Worcester, Massachusetts, newspaper looking for someone who was willing to learn clowning and to assist another clown. Since I had a theater background and was looking for something fun to do, I decided to give it a try. I thought it might be perfect for me since I was already having to commute forty-five minutes to get to Boston to work every day and I wanted something that would allow me to spend more time at home with my four-year-old son.

"I had always loved to be funny. In high school I would dress up as Harpo Marx (with a few friends filling out the Marx brothers team) and entertain at basketball games. In fact, I had seriously considered applying for the Ringling Clown College when I was eighteen, but decided that I'd better grow up and try being an adult instead. But when I started clowning, it was as if a whole new world opened up to me. I was center stage! The audience loved me. And I loved being able to make people so happy, to help them forget their worries for a few minutes.

"At first I only clowned about four or five times a month, but after more training, I fell in love with everything about being a clown and actively marketed myself so that I could clown four or five times a week.

"On a typical clown day, I spend about an hour putting in my contacts, slapping on the grease paint and combing my wig, and getting dressed. I have different bags or suitcases for each event I am doing that day. So I make sure one is packed appropriately for the job with the right magic tricks, balloons, or face paints. Sometimes I don't carry any props or balloons and just 'clown'! In any case, whatever I wish to take with me that day (including a sound system, if needed) gets loaded into the van and I'm off!

"I try not to book more than three events or a total of six hours of clowning per day and I clown anywhere from two to five days a week. Since every event is different, it is hard to predict how things will go and what will happen. I perform at birthday parties, company picnics, festivals, and motivational events. Usually the atmosphere is upbeat and fun, but the work can be very exhausting. It's like being onstage for the whole time without any backstage rest.

"As a clown, I have to be 'on' whenever I am exposed to the public. And since I'm really not following a script, I have to be thinking up the actions and dialogue constantly. So after all is done and it is time to go home and take off my clown costume, I am very tired and limp. But I almost always enjoy each and every clown moment! The only times I have ever felt danger were when someone felt that they could take liberties because I was, after all, just a clown and not a 'real' person.

"I love the expression on people's faces when they are having fun and are really into what I'm doing. Also, clowning has opened up many doors to me personally that I am sure I wouldn't have experienced otherwise. This includes being able to throw out the first pitch for our local baseball team and being part of a parade in Disney World! I have also formed many dear friendships with other clowns, which helps to keep up my desire to continue.

"What I don't like about clowning is the occasional feeling I get from some people that what I do is somehow not important or isn't a real job. They still think of professional clowning as a hobby or something you might do for Halloween. Clowns spend many hours on preparation, and like other professions, we have to keep attending classes and workshops to learn new and better techniques. We are usually very skilled not just in the technical clown skills, but also in child behavior, marketing, and management.

"Also, it is hard to get the motivation to get into makeup when I am down or sick or just don't want to work. Getting ready is quite an effort then and that's when I wish I just had a regular nine to five job and could relax on the weekends like most normal people.

"The advice I would offer to others interested in entering this field is to first contact a professional clown that you admire. If you don't have a role model, then definitely check into clown organizations such as the World Clown Association, which offers education and resources to help anyone starting or seeking to improve their clowning. Most new clowns rush into buying what they *think* they need and can't wait to get their clown feet wet, but like any other occupation, *training is essential.*"

Introducing Charlie the Clown

Charlie Stron, also known as Charlie the Clown, is a full-time entertainer based in Las Vegas, Nevada. "I always considered myself to be shy," he says. "I never thought I would be so comfortable in front of crowds.

"During high school in South Africa, I used to go to a children's youth circus group that practiced all kinds of entertainment seen in circuses," he says. "I found that I had a natural ability to juggle and balance, while 'playing.' I developed lots of circus skills and found myself enjoying the attention that I would get by doing the things I had learned.

"When I left high school I got drafted into the South African army and after basic training got transferred into the Entertainment Unit. This was a great place to practice and develop performing skills, which I later learned are more important than doing tricks. This experience in the army led me into the professional circus circuit in Europe. For two years, I worked with a flying trapeze act called the Star Lords. The following season, I did a juggling act. This led me to a show called 'Razzel Dazzle.' Later, I got a job training the actors in a musical rendition of Barnum. This production led me to another production of the same show in Portland, Oregon. I only planned on staying in the United States for three months, but I got offers and accepted a job to work as a juggler in Lake Tahoe. This led to a job in Las Vegas working for Disneyland with Ringling Brothers Circus during their production of 'Circus Fantasy' in 1996. Eventually, I immigrated and now live in Las Vegas. I also worked as a Clown College instructor for Ringling Brothers Clown College. Of course, I learned a great deal while teaching.

"At this point, I work more for myself doing birthday parties during the winter and for the summer months I do tons of fairs.

"I love my job. Not that it isn't difficult sometimes. Don't underestimate what is involved. Still, I wouldn't trade it for anything in the world. When I'm on the road, I entertain at different kinds of fairs. Part of my act consists of four one-hour shifts on stilts using different costumes. I meet and greet thousands of people, pose in pictures, make balloon animals, and juggle on the stilts. You could consider it dangerous, but—knock on wood—I have never fallen. It is a lot safer than the trapeze act I did before and pays a lot better.

"One of the greatest things about working as an entertainer is that you meet all kinds of other entertainers at different events. There is a kind of a psychological 'click.' You often meet old friends a few years down the road when you work together again.

"I like the people I work with and the contact I have with so many. However, I am not ecstatic about all the traveling. For a while, it is exciting to get paid to go and work in different places, but it can be hard to constantly be on the road.

"To be successful as a clown, you have to love people and be able to keep a big smile on your face. Remember you should be a nice guy or lady by nature and not by demand. When it really comes down to it, you've got to entertain from your heart."

Introducing Soda Pop the Clown

Rick Struve, also known as "Soda Pop," is based in Cedar Rapids, Iowa. He graduated from high school in 1982 and went to college for about two years, focusing on liberal arts and art. "Even now, I continue to take art classes whenever I can," he says.

"I have been professionally clowning since 1994," he says. "I attended four years of Clown Camp located in Wisconsin, and will be joining the staff there for the 1998 season. The majority of my actual clown training has come about through books and old-fashioned experience. And I continue to learn through clown friends when we get together. Clowns love to share information with one another.

"Each year I perform my specialties—magic, juggling, balloons, and face painting—at about 150 shows. Events range from birthday parties to company picnics to city festivals. I also run the largest clown Web site on the Internet and am head of the largest online clown newsletter. In addition, I have authored several articles for international clown magazines.

"I have always fooled around with magic, but really started reading more and more about it as I grew older. I started juggling in 1992. In 1994 I met someone who thought that I would make a good clown. He pointed me in the direction of Clown Camp, and I did my very first show the weekend after I returned—and I haven't stopped yet! Clowning came extremely natural to me, so I was able to step right into the job.

"When I was growing up, we did not have the Bozo show on TV—but we did have a local kid's show that had a costar named Mombo the Clown. This show was on the air for almost twenty-five years, and Mombo was basically the only clown I knew. He did lots of magic, and that is what first interested me in magic. I had been doing simple magic shows for my family off and on since I was eight. Then I became interested in juggling, which was a fun and relaxing hobby. When the idea of being a professional clown was put in front of me, the first thing I thought was, 'Why didn't I think of that before?' I have always loved kids, and I love to entertain whenever possible.

"I became very successful quite quickly in my area. And my biggest dream came true when I finally got to meet the man that first sparked my interest in clowning, Mombo the Clown. Now ninety-one years old, he is still a great inspiration to me. If I end up having half of the success he has had in his career, I will be a very happy clown.

"In a way, clowning is fairly unique when it comes to prior experience—you don't need any! Obviously, there are classes, books, and videos to make you a better clown, but it is all based on you. Clowning is truly in the heart—corny, but very true. Very few special people can be successful at professional clowning. Necessary talents include people skills, patience, love of children, and overcoming the fear of being in front of hundreds of people!

"As a professional clown, you are your own boss. You control everything from advertising to booking shows to paying the bills to going out to do the job.

"On a typical summer weekend, I will usually do at least three shows a day. I often get up in the morning and pack up my trunk with the items I will be using throughout the day. Then I take forty-five minutes to get my makeup on, ten minutes to get in costume, and then load everything into my van. I do my show, go back to my van, reset my trunk for the next show—and then set off again to repeat the entire process. Once all my shows are done, I drag myself home and take off the makeup and relax. Clowning can be very tiring, but you never realize it until you are off the stage—it is a great high to do a live performance.

"My normal show includes about six magic routines, one interactive song, a juggling routine, and then balloons for all the children. Sometimes I use face paints to do up the kid's faces. For larger shows I even produce a live rabbit that the children love to pet afterwards.

"During my busy season—summer—I will do an average of eight shows a week. This may only be eight to twelve hours of onstage performing, but includes a total of about thirty hours of time preparing, driving, and cleaning up afterwards.

"My work atmosphere changes with each show, and you usually don't know what it will be like until five minutes before you pop onstage! This makes things very exciting because you have to adapt to whatever situation you encounter.

"The best part of my job is when I get in front of the audience, and all attention is on me, depending on me to make them smile—I love performing. The downside of clowning for me is the time it takes to get ready for a show. Standing in front of a mirror for forty-five minutes to put on makeup, and then fifteen minutes taking it off afterwards can get very tiring.

"The advice I would offer to anyone thinking about clowning is to begin by reading books—any books that have to do with performing, or any other specific skills. Clowning has so many different aspects to it, it is very much up to the individual. If you like magic, learn as much as you can. If you like juggling, dancing, singing, puppets, balloons, anything, read up on the topic and make yourself stand out from others. I always find quality clown training extremely helpful, but the best training is to actually put your ideas in front of an audience. You will quickly learn what works for you, and what does not. Watch other clowns whenever possible—they are all different. You can pick up so much from each one. But never copy. Just learn to be the best clown you can be."

Introducing Cleggy the Clown

Jennifer Campain, also known as "Cleggy the Clown," resides in Auburn, Washington. She holds a bachelor of arts degree in sociology from Western Washington University in Bellingham.

"In addition to a *lot* of reading of library books on clowning, I continually peruse monthly newsletters from various sources," she says. "I also attend monthly educational programs at Cascade Clown Alley (Bellevue, Washington) and Clover Park Clown Alley (Tacoma, Washington), in addition to a number of ongoing clown educational seminars and other experiences. I perform intense study in many areas of clown entertainment," she stresses.

"I have a number of career titles," she says. They include:

1. Professional Clown (Cleggy the Clown)

2. Business Owner/Operator (Cleggy's Clown Company)

3. Professional Mascot (Choo-Choo the Raccoon)

4. Actress (with Kim Brooke Model and Talent) located in Seattle

"All of this was a spin-off from acting," she says. "I didn't receive enough comedy in acting roles so my husband suggested I try clowning. It sounded like a good idea to me so I began to research clowning. The rest is history.

"What attracted me most about clowning was that I had a positive image of clowns. I liked clown images and what they conveyed to me. Secondly, I have an interest in makeup and costuming. As a result, creating a clown character was great fun. Lastly and most importantly, I love to perform and make people laugh. Laughing is the single most important thing to the survival of society. We all work hard so that we are able to play. We want to laugh! I wanted to be a messenger (and reminder) of the meaning of life. I realized this when I was young.

"In the 1970s a group of educators created 'gifted programs,' schools meant to nourish the creative juices of young 'geniuses.' I was asked to attend this new program and my parents enrolled me. At this school I had the opportunity to perform in a play. I was given the role of Rumpelstiltskin. It was during that play that I realized I loved to make people laugh and could do so using my natural instinct. Oddly enough, I did not pursue drama in school or college—but the feeling never went away.

"In addition to the above statement, my training and subsequent acceptance, in 1995, into the Kim Brooke Model and Talent agency brought out the performer in me as well.

"As you can see from my many job titles, my job is quite varied. At the moment, I haven't been clowning very much due to a recent position as an official mascot for a large public market. But a typical clown day could be long or short.

"The night before a performance I do my preparations. The age and number of children and adults determines what I will do and

how long each item is performed. I will then put together a program (magic, stories, games, puppets) and pack it neatly into my
clown cooler. Clowns must always be prepared! I then prepare my
face paints (if I'm using them) and cleaning solution. If I am doing
balloons, I make sure I have enough.

"The next day, I take approximately forty-five minutes to get
completely into costume with makeup. Then I make sure I know
exactly where my destination is and leave early. Once I am on the
road, I concentrate on becoming my clown character, Cleggy the
Clown. I turn the music up, begin acting like a clown, perhaps
waving to drivers, singing to music, etc. By the time I arrive at my
destination I am relaxed and ready to entertain.

"Clown jobs can be very busy. Many times when face painting
at a public event, children line up one after another and you have
to be quick and *good!* Other times the atmosphere is relaxed. I
seem to feel less pressured during charity events. But the more I
clown, the more experienced I become and that takes the pressure
off as well.

"On one occasion I was hired for an all-day corporate picnic. It
was not busy. There was plenty of time to float from one item to
the next—but being in the persona of a clown for a long period
of time can be very hard on your body.

"A work atmosphere, for me, depends entirely on the audience
or client that hires me. If I perform for an easygoing, fun-loving
group then I enjoy myself, and actually perform better (and
longer). If the client is not very friendly or interactive, or I am
fighting off misbehaving children from my supplies and props,
then I become a little tense and lose a bit of the spirit of the
clown. I am able to work through those situations, but it takes
work and I feel very tired at the end of *that* kind of day.

"The thing I like the most about my job is making people laugh.
I enjoy bringing smiles to faces. It's as simple as that. Additionally,
I enjoy having an asset, Cleggy the Clown, that I can choose to
give to those who are underprivileged in some way. Those smiles
melt my heart.

"The thing I like least about my work is the fear of failure in succeeding to be entertaining and funny. I tend to worry before every performance about being good enough. Also, clown make-up can be very unforgiving on one's face. I have had a hard time with clown white. You must literally press it hard into your pores and chemical reactions can occur with sensitive skin such as mine. But I have been told to keep trying many brands, so I continue to do so.

"I would forward the advice that was given to me by two famous clowns: read, read, read anything you can get your hands on about clowning. Start at a library and learn all you can. Read about the history of clowning. It's important. You'll be a better clown with it. Without it you'll only be a person in costume and makeup—not a clown."

Introducing Shorty the Clown

David "Shorty" Barnett of Kansas City, Missouri, has served as secretary and president of Clowns of America International and is a member of the International Shrine Clown Association.

In 1979, he began offering his services to cheer up children in Shrine Hospital in Galveston, Texas. "Providing care for burned children without charge was very appealing to me," he says. "The clowns go to the hospital every month, and that is what I wanted to do.

"I was a professional drummer while in college and performing as a clown is much like being on stage in a band, only more personal.

"My work as a clown is a real circus—even when I'm in a hospital," he says. "I never met any grouches. Even when I was teaching clowning in a prison in Texas, everyone was friendly.

"To me, the part of clowning that I like least is getting in and out of makeup, especially taking it off. It's like losing a friend down the drain.

"I'd advise those interested in this career to follow your convictions. Study hard and practice. The kids deserve the very best that you can be. Remember you are creating a world of make-believe where fairies, cartoon characters, Peter Pan, Santa Claus, and the Easter Bunny live. Be careful not to damage a child's image of that wonderful world of make-believe."

Introducing Mama Clown and Friends

Mama Clown heads Mama Clown and Friends, a full-service party and event planning company. Mama Clown, also known as Marcella Murad, attended Broward Community College for two years, then attended Clown Camp at the University of Wisconsin. She also has completed advanced studies in the art of clowning and attended Laughmakers Conferences and numerous conventions and seminars. A native of Colombia, South America, she has lived the life of her alter ego, Mama Clown, since 1978. Twice elected Clown of the Year by the Southeast Clown Association, Mama Clown was honored with a cover story in the October 1996 issue of *Calliope*, the official magazine of Clowns of America International. She was also featured on the nationally syndicated *Cristina Show* and has won numerous awards for her contributions to the art of clowning. She is a writer for *Laughmakers* magazine.

In order to help others become clowns (or better clowns), she will be offering the following seminars this year: Face Painting, Advanced Fantasy Makeup, Hand Painted Jewelry and Tattoos, Birthday Parties, Silk Magic, Comedy Magic, Fun and Practical Balloons, Comedy Patter for Children, Storytelling, Audience Participation, Theme Shows, Character Development, Clowning Without Props, Basic Spanish for Entertainers, Performing with Store-Bought Toys, Close-up Magic, Clown Style, and Music—the Universal Language.

Silly Farm Products distributes clown supplies to the trade and manufactures Mama's own line of magic and props. Mama's book,

Put On A Happy Face: The Complete Book of Face Painting, has become a mainstay for professional face painters. She has been called a "Home-Town Hero" by the *Miami Herald* for her work with the Cuban refugee children and an "Angel of Cheer" by the Associated Press for giving so much of her time to comfort those affected by Hurricane Andrew.

"My clowning began twenty years ago, when I decided (out of nowhere) to theme my children's birthday party with clowns," explains Marcella. "I hired a 'professional' who was not well trained and decided I could do better. Throughout my career I had many lucky breaks and wonderful opportunities for advancement.

"To live my life performing as a clown is not something that I planned. It kind of happened little by little as I learned to love what I do with all my heart. It didn't take long to realize how lucky I am to have found a career that pays me to act like a child, make a difference in a child's life, and lift people's spirits. I have always been an easygoing person with a good sense of humor. Clowning came very naturally to me and in twenty years of clowning, not once have I wished to be doing something else.

"After graduating from high school, I spend two years at a junior college. Then I got married. When my first child was born, I became a full-time housewife and mother.

"Before that I was a waitress. My children became like my real-life dolls. I loved playing with them, telling them stories, and making crafts with them. They taught me how to love children and that has been a big plus in my career.

"I honestly believe I have the best job in the world. Whether I'm performing, writing articles for clown magazines or books on the subject, creating new products, or traveling as an instructor, most anything I do in my life is related to clowning. You can say that somehow I work all day long but to me it is not work because I love what I do so much.

"There's very little stress factor in my job. My sister, Claudia Banks, who is now co-owner of our party-planning company, does all the bookings and deals with the clients and event preparations. (Now, she has stress!) My oldest daughter Jessica takes care of our mail-order business and watches over my cats while I'm away on business. I get contracted often as a speaker and instructor at conventions, camps, and seminars across the country and in Mexico and Puerto Rico.

"A typical weekday for me starts at 7:00 A.M. with breakfast and a visit to the gym. Then I try to do at least half the things on my never ending list. That could include taking mail orders to the post office or United Parcel Service, finishing an article with a deadline, writing a new show, preparing for a show, or actually performing a show. On a typical weekend, I entertain at an average of four events a day. This is exhausting because it takes so much energy but is extremely rewarding to be part of all the celebrations.

"What I love the most about my job are the smiles and friendliness that my character brings out in children of all ages. I love my work because it is so much fun and it keeps me young at heart. There aren't many downfalls except maybe the few times when I encounter rude people or when I see children in pain.

"When I was married and my children were younger, the fact that I worked weekends created stress in the household. And during crises in my own life, such as during my divorce, it was hard to be up when I was hurting so much inside, but in the long run, it ended up being the best therapy for me.

"My advice to others is to make sure you honestly like children. They have a sixth sense and can tell if you are sincere. They will react to you according to the vibes they sense coming from you.

"You must love what you do with all your heart and success will follow. It is not easy becoming a performer. You need a lot of dedication to ensure that you achieve your goals.

"Many people think that to be a clown all you need are baggy clothes, a big pair of shoes, some makeup, and a business card. Nothing can be further from the truth. Clowning is an art that takes a lifetime to master. Being funny is a serious business and becoming a professional takes time and a large investment of your time and money.

Introducing Shadow the Clown

Shadow the Clown, also known as Kathy Lange, earned a bachelor of arts in education at Central Washington University, Ellensburg, Washington, in 1987. Her major was elementary education with an early childhood education emphasis. Combining a love for children with clowning, she took Fundamentals of Clowning at Bellevue Community College in Bellevue, Washington, attended Clown Camp at Medicine Hat in Alberta, Canada, and participated in the Northwest Festival of Clowns, held in various locations in the Pacific Northwest in September of each year. She also tries to attend local workshops and conventions each year to gain new knowledge and skills. "I do this to keep things fresh and new," she says. "It is an ongoing educational process.

"Most people who know me aren't all that surprised that I now put on makeup to be a clown," says Shadow. "I have always been one to be a bit goofy at times. Ask my dad what his nickname for me has always been, and he'll answer 'Ding-y!'

"I always loved working with children. My first job out of college was with a gymnastics facility that worked with children in a noncompetitive atmosphere. The program was designed to provide skills not just for gymnastics but for fitness, exercise, and self-esteem. We used a lot of music and games in our format and I would dress up in silly costumes during theme weeks we would create. I had the best time making up themes, stories, and costumes!

"When I left my gymnastics job after four years, I needed an outlet to be creative and still work with young children, so I finally took the class I had been eyeing for two years in the college course catalog. Shadow was born.

"Being a clown gives me, as an adult, the freedom to walk and talk silly, to make people laugh just by dressing up and making funny faces. It allows me to make a child who might be going through troubled times smile and forget, even for just a few moments, the pain and despair of his or her condition. It might allow me to be remembered from a hospital visit, a parade, or any other venue I might be doing. One of the greatest feelings for me is when a child will come up to you and say, 'Hey, I remember you, you did [such and such a thing] and it was funny!' Or 'Shadow, you're so silly!' It makes them smile and it's a great gift to be able to do that.

"Why a clown? Well, one thing that had a great influence on me was growing up as the youngest and only girl with three brothers! Seriously, I think my genetic makeup has a lot to do with it. The easiest thing for me in life has always been to take care of children. Something in me understands them, knows what they are feeling, and makes me go to their level to talk to them and entertain them. I baby-sat extensively when I was a teenager, and loved to do that more than anything else. I worked in a recreation department in my hometown for five summers teaching tennis and arts and crafts to young children, working with the special education day camp. I worked in a girls' camp in upstate New York after that for two summers. Then there was the job I mentioned above in a noncompetitive gymnastics facility for four years. After the gymnastics facility, I became an insurance assistant for two years. It was not a job I wanted for long, but it did make me jump into the clowning business because I needed a creative outlet. To me, insurance can be very stale. It was the first and only job I had that did not include working around or with children.

"I am not a full-time clown. I do have a day job. As a full-time job, and sole source of income, clowning would be very stressful for me. There are those who can do it, and I envy them in some ways but I am too practical and not a big enough risk taker to forego a steady paycheck. I want clowning to stay fun and not be too worrisome. I also need a lot of variety in my life, which includes many things besides clowning.

"A typical Saturday in the busy season (spring and summer) may include a parade with the club I belong to. I have to be up pretty early to get makeup and costume on. It takes about an hour (not including eating breakfast, taking a shower, etc., and driving). We meet for the parade, usually an hour or more before it starts, and entertain the other parade participants while waiting in line. After the parade I may be finished for the day and may go home and review the tricks or things we did in the parade to figure out if they worked or not. Or I may have a birthday party to attend. That would include a whole new set of props and tricks because then I would be putting on a small show and giving away things like candy and Shadow coloring pages.

"The atmosphere in clowning is what you make it, and it also really depends on the type of gig you are doing. A parade is relaxed and fast paced as you are moving down the route and doing the same trick over and over to a constantly changing audience. A birthday party can be relaxed or pretty crazy depending on the age and manners of the party attendees. A company picnic, which I love to do a lot in the summer, is usually relaxed and steady moving.

"A typical day for a picnic starts out early getting all the necessary props together, and combining them in hopefully a small enough package that you aren't making too many trips back and forth to the car once you get there. A red wagon comes in very handy!

"At a picnic I usually combine face painting, balloon twisting, and games. A clown is typically there to entertain the children. Usually the adults have their own games planned for them or they like to sit and talk while enjoying music. Face painting at a company picnic is a good beginner as people are arriving. It is a nonthreatening way for the clown to get to know the kids. Some of the younger ones aren't always sure about a clown right away. Walking around before anything organized starts and handing out stickers is also good. Games consist of relays, water balloon tossing, parachute games, or they can get more complicated with more props and supplies. It's up to the company who hires you or how far your imagination will take you. Balloon twisting is a good way to end, as the kids wind down, and so does the clown. I make all sorts of balloon animals, hats, flowers, etc. And even some of the adults will want their faces painted or a balloon twisted. It's not all just for kids!

"I like the camaraderie with the children most. They can take to you so easily. There isn't the suspicion as there can be in adults. Children let you know right away if they like you or not and it is easier to change their minds about you.

"I enjoy the creativeness it takes to be a clown, the constant change in finding things that are new, and the ability to put a smile on a face. In a hospital setting, the ability to make a child who may be hurting forget for just a few minutes and smile is very rewarding. I also enjoy the crazy look you see on people's faces when you tell them you are a clown, usually an instant smile and maybe a little envy that they wish they had the personality to be a clown. I love the pure fun of it, to be totally uninhibited, in a good way, when in makeup. Society places constraints on people as we grow up and being a clown is a vehicle to still act like a child but avoid being ridiculed for not acting your age!

"What I like least are pushy parents, those who think their child should not be afraid of a clown so they push the child to accept a clown before he or she is ready to do so. To young children, a clown can be terrifying no matter how friendly that clown is. This could be just because the clown is a stranger and children often view strangers as frightening. If children are allowed to warm up to a clown in their own time, they are more likely to start enjoying the clown and not feel threatened. The parents need to see it from the child's point of view, not their own.

"I would advise people to go for it! Look around in your local area for classes, attend workshops, go to Clown Camp, learn, learn, learn. Don't think makeup and a costume are the only things you need. You need skills, patience, a love for entertaining, and a love for children. Make sure your clown face is inviting and your costume is neat and colorful. Once you get started, always look to improve. Make things fresh for you and the people you are entertaining. Don't just do it for the money—visit hospitals, nursing homes, retirement centers. The people who reside there especially need cheering up and entertainment to break up the day, and it can be a great pick-me-up for you, too. Laughter is the best medicine. Just have fun!"

> *Here's another birth name challenge:*
> Joseph Levitch

For More Information

The International Clown Hall of Fame and Research Center, Inc., is dedicated to the preservation and advancement of clown art. Represented by professional and amateur clown associations, it pays tribute to outstanding clown performers, operates a living museum of clowning with resident clown performers, conducts special events, and maintains a national archive of clown artifacts and history.

Clowns of America International (COAI) is a great resource for learning about becoming a clown and other aspects of clowning. Informative articles regarding makeup, costuming, props, skit development, etc., are provided through the official publication, called "The New Calliope," which is published six times a year. Membership in the organization includes a spring international convention and other benefits. Membership is open to individuals sixteen and older.

Other Organizations

American Guild of Variety Artists
184 Fifth Avenue
New York, NY 10019

Associated Actors and Artists of America
165 West 46th Street
New York, NY 10036

Ringling Brothers and Barnum and Bailey Clown College
P. O. Box 1528
Venice, FL 34284-1528

Books

Be a Clown by Mark Stolzenberg. Sterling Publications, 1989. A treasure chest of ideas and skits that will help you develop your clown and your routines. Several well-scripted skits, including "The Whipcracker," "The Boxing Gag," and "The Washerwoman."

Be a Clown! With Red Ball Nose by Turk Pipkin, Walt Chrynwski, and Chris Reed. Workman Publishing Co., 1989. A delightful guide full of impressive tips: balancing a Ping-Pong ball on your nose, a flea circus, and napkin rabbits. There are plenty of notes on famous clowns, costumes, and makeup tips.

Clown Act Omnibus: Everything You Need to Know About Clowning Plus over 200 Clown Stunts by Wes McVicar. Meriwether Publishers, 1987.

Punny Stuff by Happy De Klown. This booklet contains prop drawings and one-liners to use in your acts. Write to Happy De Klown, 3930 Capri, Corpus Christi, TX 78415.

Strutter's Complete Guide to Clown Makeup by Jim Roberts. Piccadilly Books, 1991. The definitive guide to learning how to apply makeup for the three basic clown types: Whiteface, Auguste, and Hobo/Tramp. Step-by-step photographic lessons for each type, from preparing your skin, applying the makeup, powdering, and nose application. Chapters on noses, wigs, and makeup problems provide valuable lessons. The concluding gallery provides forty-five full-color examples of makeup as used by the clowns.

CHAPTER THREE

Comedians

"Laugh and the world laughs with you; weep and you weep alone."
ELLA WHEELER WILCOX

T o stand before an audience, tell a joke, and have the laughter explode around me is the most exciting thrill I know," says Robert Henry, humorist. But it takes lots of work for this to happen. The comedian creates the illusion that comedy is effortless. He or she does this by practicing his or her routine over and over.

Zeroing in on What a Comedian Does

It's no surprise that a comedian's job is to make people laugh. How they do this may be accomplished in a number of ways. Comedians are entertainers who perform monologues or skits, tell jokes, deliver comic lines, sing humorous songs, perform comedic dances or walks, wear funny costumes, do impersonations, and use bodily movements and facial contortions to try to make audiences react by laughing.

Comedians who work in nightclubs are often called stand-up comedians. They try to entertain audiences with stories, jokes, one-liners, and impressions. In comedy clubs in large cities, they may do more than one show a night, and go on either before or after another comedian. Depending on whether they are the opening act or the main act, they perform sets of material that are anywhere from ten minutes to an hour or longer.

Stand-up comedians may work alone like Jerry Seinfeld or in pairs like the Smothers Brothers. When they work in pairs, one usually takes the part of the "straight man" (or woman) who appears to speak in a serious manner. The other person feeds off that individual in a humorous way.

Comedians may entertain audiences in nightclubs, halls, conventions, hotel parties, indoor and outdoor festivals, private parties, theaters, and at concerts. Comedy clubs provide avenues for young comics to hone their talents before live audiences.

After comedians have sharpened their acts, they may be asked to appear on television on a talk show or a comedy special. Some comedians complete comedy concerts that are videotaped and broadcast. If comedians become really well known, they may have a television series developed for them.

It's What You Say and How You Say It

Most comedians write their own material (and sometimes material for other comedians). And a lot of it is needed since professional joke tellers suggest a one-joke-a-minute guideline. Usually, the humor is created and built from people and situations around them—often ordinary, everyday items like toothpaste and candy. After the material is written, comedians usually study it, trying to absorb it and envision how they will act it out onstage. Then they will practice aloud to establish timing and rhythm. Most comics perform from memory, though a few use notes or other aids.

Many comedians critique their own performances by videotaping them and then studying them carefully. Then it is time to try a live audience, perhaps at either a dinner party or in front of a friendly crowd of family, friends, or acquaintances.

The final step for the comedian is the moment of performance. To be successful at this job, you must enjoy being the center of attention under difficult circumstances. You must be able to recall your planned material while you are analyzing the audience's feedback and making instant adjustments to keep the laughs coming. It takes a combination of solid material and personal charm to have a winning formula for success.

A comedian develops a unique style, skill, and body of work as an entertainer. Jim Carrey, Robin Williams, Whoopi Goldberg all have very distinctively different comedic styles and they have all enjoyed great success.

Comedy Troupes

Comedy troupes develop, perform, and publicize their own material. Most of the members maintain freelance or day jobs which allow them to pursue this career. They usually schedule a weekly show, bracketed around rehearsal and workshops where they critique each other's sketches and performances.

Because audiences will not return to see the same material, it is a highly pressured large-output environment. A troupe comedian must adapt to peers' comments and take criticism well. The ability to work with others is also critical to success.

The troupes are often formed in major urban centers, like Chicago or New York, where many actors and comedians congregate because there are greater opportunities to find work.

The Road to Comedy

Comedians come from all walks of life. Some hold bachelor's or graduate degrees. Others have not even graduated from high school. There are no formal education requirements. However, advanced learning is definitely a plus in this line of work. It gives you a much broader base of knowledge to draw humor from. Course work in drama, communications, speech, theater, English, composition, business, broadcasting, and public speaking are all advantageous (both at the high school and college level).

Seminars, workshops, and courses in comedy performance and writing are also helpful. These may be offered through many types of schools as either credit or noncredit classes.

Comedians need to be able to perform a variety of tasks, must know how to deal with people, and should have a pleasant speaking voice. In addition, a successful comedian must be quick-witted, able to think on his or her feet, dedicated, and lucky. A great deal of self-confidence is required if one is to last over two years in this profession (and over half don't), since failure, disappointment, and rejection are standard.

The Reality—Paying Your Dues

Paying your dues may mean performing in dingy nightclubs before an audience of one and walking away without a penny to show for it. Stand-up comedians have a more uncertain road than troupe comedians, going from club to club, writing material, practicing and refining it, and hoping for a break.

It is not unusual for aspiring stand-up comics to log over two hundred days per year away from home, traveling from city to city, entertaining different types of audiences and sharpening their acts in the process. To book these out-of-town performances, the comedians may call the club owners themselves or go through a booking agent. In medium- and small-sized cities, they will perform only one night and then drive or fly to the next city.

While it can be a glamorous profession, comedians also face many difficulties. They are away from home for most of the year. They are also very vulnerable. Comedians go onstage alone and if they don't make the crowd laugh, they have no one to blame but themselves. But when the audience does laugh, comedians feel richly rewarded.

Moving Up and Making It

It is much easier for comedians to advance in their careers now than it was even only ten years ago. Comedy clubs are popular throughout the country. Almost every city has at least one club. There are also a large number of opportunities to appear on television, whether it be on local, network, independent, or cable station shows.

Some comedians stop working stand-up and go on to perform in situation comedies or films. The long list of performers who have successfully accomplished this includes Sinbad, Jerry Seinfeld, Roseanne, Robin Williams, Eddie Murphy, and Bill Cosby. Other comedians such as Joan Rivers, Chevy Chase, Jay Leno, and Jenny Jones have gone on to host television talk shows.

Success takes incredible perseverance. Comics must cope with rejection, criticism, and low pay while launching their careers. Comics naturally develop a style of humor that is suited to them, but finding the right niche can take years.

Competition among comedians is intense. Ten thousand comedians compete nightly for the opportunity to appear on one of seven hundred comedy stages. But new opportunities are arising—some companies, for example, are hiring comedians for seminars designed to provide stress management.

Compensation for Comedians

Working stand-up comedians may either get paid by the show or for a week of performances. The headliner makes much more than the opening act.

In large comedy clubs in the nation's major cities, a headliner can earn from $1,000 to $20,000 per week, depending on his or her popularity. The comedian who opens the evening's show can earn from $150 to $300 per week, while the middle comedian can earn from $400 to $800 per week.

At the beginning, comedians often work just to get the experience, exposure, and to make valuable contacts. They may also perform for "the door," which means they receive part of the admission price paid by the people who attended the show.

For comedy writers, the pay scale is also very wide. Those who write jokes for famous comedians usually get paid around $50 for every joke used. Those who write for television get paid different rates depending on their experience, reputation, and the budget of the show. The writers of a network comedy show can be paid anywhere from $50,000 to $150,000 or more a year.

Tips for Success

Here are some tips for those of you who would like to pursue comedy as a career:

- Take classes and workshops in performing and writing comedy.

- Participate in comedy "competitions," which are offered throughout the country, often sponsored by television stations, comedy clubs, and/or corporate sponsors. Try to get involved with these programs. They are excellent ways to obtain exposure.

- Offer to emcee any type of entertainment event you can find. Consider local talent and variety shows, telethons, charity dinners, luncheons, etc.

- Take part in local talent and variety shows.

- Perform as often as you can to hone your skills, obtain experience, and perfect your act.

- Believe in yourself! A great deal of success in this field is based upon not only talent, but drive, determination, ambition, and perseverance. Don't give up.

- Go to clubs and watch other comedians perform. Observe what makes their acts successful.

- Watch comedians who perform on television. Check out their styles, techniques, timing, and content.

- When you and your act are ready, try to get a paying job in comedy. Remember—make sure you are ready!

- Locate all nightclubs and comedy clubs in your area and find out the requirements for performing. Many have amateur or open mike nights as well as talent showcases where new entertainers can try out material and hone their acts.

- Consider talking to local bands, singers, and other musical acts about opening for them.

- When you are ready, contact agents who specialize in booking comedy acts.

Words from the Pros

Introducing Randy Judkins

Randy Judkins received a bachelor of science degree in secondary education–mathematics at the University of Southern Maine and took some master's classes at Wesleyan University in Connecticut. He has studied acting, circus arts, and mime and has served as a part-time college professor. He now serves as an "EDUtrainer"—an inspirational speaker and performer.

Things fell into place for Randy in phases. "The first phase began in 1975. I simply wanted to write, book, and tour my one-man (sometimes silent) character comedy show," he says.

"The second phase occurred in 1990 when I discovered a technique for blending interactive entertainment with research on human resource topics like change, team building, humor, and self-esteem.

"I actually love being onstage, making people laugh. Consequently my mission has been to diversify enough to reach as many sectors of society as possible.

"It seems that my experiences as a young person from a large family and a close-knit neighborhood contributed to my playful attitude towards my work onstage and with people in general. Also I am grateful for the years I spent in summer camp, not as much for the roles I played as a Boy Scout, an assistant chef, a wilderness camp trip leader, and a YMCA program director, but more for the opportunities it has presented to me to perform.

"My job has many facets to it. On one day I may drive for one to three hours to present for a group of teachers at a staff development day. Another day will see me hopping a plane to Houston to keynote a conference on wellness topics like laughter. Yet another day is made up of working in my office following up referrals, developing new clients, booking flights to Wisconsin, Georgia, Florida, Iowa, or to ten other states to work with businesses as diverse as Ralston Purina Company and the Medical Group Management Association.

"I spend from forty to fifty hours per week doing what I love to do. Most of my clients present me with an outstanding working atmosphere. When the environment is sub-par, I can usually shift enough things around (including my own thinking) to produce a successful event.

"I truly love the interaction with my audiences. In fact I often create sketches that enable me to involve the audience on many different levels. Most of the time they are playfully invested within seconds.

"The downside of this career is my having to constantly do all of the legwork needed to line up all the engagements. (I could use a good agent or manager!)

"My advice to others would be to get out there and work—first for just the experiences and little pay. As your reputation grows, if it does (and you still love doing it), then it may be possible for you to carve out your niche, set some short- and long-term goals, and get some support for the skills you need to pull it all off. *Go for it.*"

Introducing Bob Crawford

When Bob Crawford earned a master's degree in photography, he planned to put it to good use. Well, he still does sometimes, working as a freelance computer graphics artist. But in September 1994, in a small comedy club in Birmingham, Alabama, he was encouraged to get onstage during open mike night, and he's been touring the country as a professional comedian ever since.

Bob says that just living his life—and having the ability to pay close attention to what happens—has given him the additional training he needs to be successful, because he has "lived life on the wild side and been lucky enough to have survived to tell about it." He also believes that the many different jobs he has held in his life have helped him widen his points of view on life.

He has worked as a truck driver, tattoo artist, vacuum cleaner salesman, bartender, and more. "I've managed to find the introspective vision to look back and, in spite of the pain and joy of living, find humor in the collective experience," he says.

"At a young age, I was exposed to Bill Cosby, Richard Pryor, and others. By nature, I'm a showoff and a clown—a good combination for this business. Crowds don't intimidate me; the more the better. I love to entertain people, and inducing laughter in people is a true high for me.

"When I'm on the road, I'm usually exploring the town or, if I've been there before, I'm hanging out with old friends or just finding a decent coffee shop to read the paper and relax. I always make it a point to find out as much about the local color as I can; there's always an opportunity to work recent local events into a show. Back in my room, at least a few hours before show time, I'm getting ready for work—reading material and making mental notes about the area, working out what the first thing out of my mouth will be when I hit the stage. A famous comic once told me, 'There are only two things that make a great stage performance in comedy: the first thing out of your mouth and the last thing out of your mouth. The rest is just filler.'

"Once at the club, it's time to find the 'green room'—the area where the comics hang out while the show goes on. I watch and listen to the audience as much as possible. It comes in handy later and quite often forces a change in that opening line. When the show is over, I like to hang out with the people leaving; making friends out of the audience can't hurt anyone's career. Often the comics will get together at a local coffee shop or bar to catch up on news or gossip.

"The most fun about being a comedian is that moment when you realize that you have an audience on your side. An old Chinese proverb says, 'It takes no skill to hurt people, but great skill to make them laugh,' and I subscribe to that wholeheartedly. The money is great, too, and if you like to travel like me, then it's even better. The 'road' is a strange place in comedy. You meet the rising stars and the fallen would-be's.

"The most difficult part of this career is being away from home and family at times when I'd rather not be. Another bothersome factor is a club owner who won't talk to you and let you know exactly what the establishment is looking for in a performance.

"Comedy isn't a career choice for the majority of us—we tend to back into it. It's something that you discover in yourself and realize that you don't mind sharing with a roomful of strangers. It's the adrenaline rush of hearing the audience applaud a line that you knew would get them, but still had some doubt.

"If you have a fragile ego and a weak heart, don't do this kind of work. If having people shout 'You stink!' from the black hole that exists in the back of the room will make you angry, you're in for a lot of troubled nights. Lastly, if you fear failure and rejection and can't handle indulging people as they share their innermost thoughts about why you're just not funny, stay away.

"However, if you enjoy the limelight, being the center of attention, and being your own absolute boss, then go for it. It's a big world and your viewpoint just might strike a funny bone out there somewhere."

Here is your next birth name challenge:
Joan Alexandra Molinsky

For More Information

Organizations

Aspiring comedians may contact the following organizations to learn more about careers in this field:

American Federation of Television and Radio Artists (AFTRA)
260 Madison Avenue
New York, NY 10016

American Guild of Variety Artists (AGVA)
184 Fifth Avenue
New York, NY 10010

Comedy Writers/Performers Association
P. O. Box 023304
Brooklyn, NY 11202-0066

National Comedians' Association (NCA)
581 Ninth Avenue, Suite 3-C
New York, NY 10036
(Formerly Professional Comedians Association)

Books

Be a Clown! by Turk Pipkin. Workman Publishing, 1989.

Comedy Writing for Television and Hollywood by Milt Josefsberg. Harper and Row, 1987.

Comedy Writing Secrets by Melvin Helitzer. Writer's Digest Books, 1985.

Comic Lives by Betsy Borns. Simon & Schuster, 1987.

The Craft of Comedy Writing by Sol Saks. Writer's Digest Books, 1985.

How to Be a Stand-Up Comic by Richard Belzer. Villard Books, 1988.

How to Hold Your Audience with Humor by Gene Perret. Writer's Digest Books, 1984.

How to Write and Sell Your Sense of Humor by Gene Perret. Writer's Digest Books, 1982.

Stand-Up Comedy: The Book by Judy Carter. Dell Publishing, 1989.

2100 Laughs for all Occasions by Robert Orben. Doubleday & Company, 1972.

CHAPTER FOUR

Jugglers and More

"Always laugh when you can. It is cheap medicine." LORD BYRON

How many balls can you keep in the air at one time? Most of us feel we are keeping considerably more than we'd like to—pushed around by the fast-paced existence we call contemporary life. Not literally, of course, but figuratively. We go to see performances by jugglers to show us how to do it literally.

Jugglers are considered *variety performers*, a group that also includes mimes, impersonators, ventriloquists, puppeteers, storytellers, clowns, comedians, and magicians.

Jugglers may entertain audiences by working alone or in groups. They may present their acts in many ways and styles in order to meet the interests and tastes of their audiences. Performers may do a single show, or they may present a complete show in nightclubs, circuses, fairs, carnivals, motion pictures, or television.

What's It Like to Be a Juggler?

Jugglers may have to perform under all kinds of conditions. They may work indoors or outdoors, at night or in the daytime. They may perform in a major theater, in a school auditorium, or in the parking lot of a shopping center.

Nightclubs may be crowded and noisy. Studios may be hot and poorly ventilated. Gymnasiums may have no stage or poor sound systems. Conventions and trade shows can be noisy and distracting. Entertainers must be able to adjust to whatever situation is at hand.

Successful jugglers are usually required to travel. Many entertainers travel an established circuit. They wedge rest and meals between travel and performances. When they are first starting, performers may have little time or money for meals and hotel rooms.

Few entertainers work regular hours. A performance may be anything from a ten-second television commercial to a full-length performance lasting several hours. They may contract for a single appearance or for a long engagement of several weeks. Besides performing, they spend time each day in practice and rehearsals. A one-hour television show may require five days of rehearsal.

What Does Juggling Require?

Jugglers should have talent, stage presence, and self-confidence in order to establish a rapport with the audience. Stamina, self-discipline, commitment, and the determination to keep trying are also vital. So are strength, endurance, flexibility, coordination, and dexterity.

Since performers have to sell themselves to agents, employers, and their audiences, they must have charm, style, and originality. They must also be able to work well with their coperformers, technicians, directors, and others, and they need to be able to adapt to a constantly changing schedule as well as the stress of a scarcity of bookings.

Training

There are no defined educational requirements for performers. However, a good academic background is important. High school subjects should include English, the arts, and business courses. A college degree is always a strong asset. Many colleges offer programs in theater arts, which include interpretation, costumes, makeup, history, directing, and related studies.

Jugglers do need to study and practice their craft. All successful performers have worked long and hard to perfect their skills.

Students who want to be performers can start developing their skills in grade school. They should appear in school plays and shows and perform at parties, for church and community audiences, and in talent contests.

Finding a Good Place to Juggle

Jugglers may work in a variety of places. The main centers for the highest-paid workers are New York, Hollywood, and Las Vegas. All large cities have stadiums, arenas, and other entertainment centers. Small towns and rural regions have schools and churches. Performers may work in private homes, on street corners, or in shopping malls. They may also work in nightclubs, casinos, hotels, resorts, and restaurants. They perform for business meetings, conventions, promotions, and industrial and trade shows. They work at a wide range of social events and private parties.

Schools and colleges also offer some possibilities. Performers appear for fraternities and sororities, alumni groups, special interest groups, class reunions, and student bodies. College theater groups also employ variety performers.

Organizations of all kinds book performers for meetings, fundraisers, children's parties, seasonal and holiday shows, parades, and other social and business events. Performers may find work at festivals, pageants, and fairs. They may travel with a carnival or circus, or on a cruise ship.

Performers may tour other countries as part of a company, or with a USO group. They may appear in stage shows, at dinner theaters, in motion pictures, and in television shows and commercials. City parks, recreation departments, and amusement parks may hire jugglers.

The Road to Juggling

Many performers start out in local charity or school programs. They may appear on talent shows. As they become better known, they audition for booking agents, producers, and other employers.

Trade journals list jobs. The yellow pages list theatrical agencies and booking agents. Performers may get leads through a union or from friends and associates. They can make phone calls, write letters, and send resumes to potential employers. They must have a portfolio and possibly videotapes to show prospective employers their record of performances.

Beginning variety performers in New York and other major cities may develop their acts in clubs, cabarets, and places that offer an open mike. Some entertainers perform on the street or at festivals.

Performers have no guarantee of promotions or higher pay. Those with talent, determination, and luck may find openings. Performers who become known locally may hire an agent to get bookings. A few may become celebrities. Others may be satisfied with steady work. Successful performers may continue as a solo act, or they may start their own company and advance to directing and producing. They may work as promoters or agents for other performers.

Compensation for Jugglers

The earnings of jugglers vary with their skill, fame, employer, geographic region, and the kind and amount of work. They may receive anywhere from $25 to $10,000 a performance. Median fees range from $100 to $1,000, and weekly salaries range from $500 to $1,400. Some entertainers earn more for an hour than others do for a week, but the pay for that one hour may be all they get for a month.

Minimum union scale for five performances, set by the American Guild of Variety Artists, is basically $150 a day, for one to eight hours of work, and $300 a week, for six shows. Self-employed jugglers may negotiate for earnings and working conditions.

Those in film work, both television and motion pictures, may earn as little as $100 a day, or up to $1,250 a week. These fees are set by the Screen Actors Guild and the American Federation of Television and Radio Artists. Individuals can bargain for more.

Union contracts set terms for overtime and residuals (payment for reruns of films, commercials, and television shows in which the performers appear). The performers may also get a percentage of any sales from videos or other items such as dolls and games modeled after these performers.

Since most performers are self-employed, they do not receive the fringe benefits other workers get. Although they work nights, weekends, and holidays, they seldom get extra pay. Union contracts may include pension plans, health insurance, and other aid. Entertainers who work for one employer long enough can collect unemployment insurance when the job ends. Sick leave and paid vacations are rare. National and local arts organizations sometimes offer group insurance and other benefits for those not covered by union contracts.

Most performers have other work. Many take whatever kind of work they can get to fill in between jobs. They may sell their tapes, films, books, or other products.

Always Be a Professional

Most professional entertainers belong to one or more labor unions. The American Guild of Variety Artists represents performers in nightclubs, circuses, and other places that present live entertainment. The American Federation of Television and Radio

Artists serves performers of live or taped radio and television programs.

The Screen Actors Guild serves performers in film, television, and commercials. The American Federation of Musicians serves instrumentalists. The Associated Actors and Artists of America is an umbrella organization for the nine AFL-CIO unions that represent performing artists. All these unions negotiate contracts on wages, hours, and working conditions. Performers may sign individual contracts with special terms.

International Jugglers Association

The premier organization for jugglers is the International Jugglers Association (IJA), founded in 1947. It is the nonprofit organization uniquely dedicated to the advancement and promotion of juggling worldwide. The IJA membership represents an incredibly diverse array of skills, ages, and interests, and spans the range from amateurs to dedicated professionals. It is open to all who seek to share their love of juggling.

The organization's mission is to educate and render assistance to fellow jugglers. They wish to provide an accessible source of information pertaining to juggling and jugglers and to record and maintain the history of juggling.

The IJA offers a wide variety of tools, including an annual festival and winter mini-festival. The summer festival is the big one and is usually held in late July or early August. The winter festival is a smaller, less structured event held in early January in Las Vegas, Nevada, at the Showboat Hotel and Casino. Recently the IJA added its Fun-in-the-Sun festival in Key West, Florida. This is a free festival and is even less structured than the winter festival.

The organization also produces videotapes of its events and instructional material which members may purchase. *Juggler's World* magazine is published quarterly by the IJA, presenting reviews of new videos, books and props; reviews and descriptions of some of history's great juggling acts; interviews with the juggling world's most fascinating personalities; historical information, and more.

What Does the Future Hold?

The outlook for jobs in the entertainment field is limited and uncertain. There is no accurate estimate of the number of performers or the number of jobs available. The unemployment rate is very high—60 to 65 percent for these workers. The competition is stiff. The number of job seekers is always greater than the number of jobs.

Most entertainers work only part-time. At best they make only a modest living. Only a few become rich and famous.

Words from the Pros

Introducing the Raspyni Brothers

The Raspyni Brothers are not actually brothers, but they are a successful juggling duo. Dan Holzman and Barry Friedman first met in a park when they were twenty years old, and they quickly formed a partnership to perform comedy/juggling shows for the summer of 1982. Sixteen years later, their credits include *The Tonight Show* and "Command Performance for the President." They have also performed as the opening act for Tom Jones, Robin Williams, Billy Crystal, and other famous entertainers. They have the distinction of being the only two-time International Juggling Champions.

"We were both very passionate about performing and juggling," they share. "We started at a young age and gave ourselves specific goals that we had to either achieve, or quit. Each time a goal or deadline got close, we would achieve it. That tradition continues today."

For their previous jobs, Dan sat in a room and sorted X rays. Barry drove a forklift in a small warehouse. "These jobs had a tremendous bearing on our career paths, because we knew that if we didn't find something more interesting and challenging to do with our lives, they would just bring us more X rays and pallets.

"Now, we spend most of our time on airplanes flying around the country. Well, that's not entirely true—we also fly internationally. On show days, we meet with clients and make sure that we understand exactly what they are expecting from us as performers.

"Then we tell them what they are going to get from us as performers, and hopefully the two visions are similar.

"On at-home days we meet and talk about new markets, new routines, and new projects we can pursue to make ourselves more popular. We also practice juggling an hour each day. We are both working on playing musical instruments and hope to incorporate these skills into our show in the very near future. The name of our game is having people call and say, 'I want to hire the Raspyni Brothers' and not 'I want to hire a juggling act.' Whatever gets us to that end is what fills our days.

"What do we like? The travel, the money, the excitement of performing, meeting and working with famous celebrities (because it humanizes them and makes their level seem attainable to us), being on television, seeing new places, staying in world-class resorts, getting standing ovations, seeing people laugh so hard that they have tears in their eyes, doing encores, sending postcards from the Caribbean to all the people who said we'd never make anything of ourselves, and eating in New Orleans.

"What are the downsides? Many of the same things from above could go here! Seriously, the only downside is being away from home so much. Our life is the textbook case of 'the greener grass' theory. We usually find ourselves either at home or on the road and wishing for the other. Too often, friends get married on weekends when we are traveling. Too bad more people don't get married on Tuesday nights; we're usually available!

"Our advice is to work hard and to be creative. Don't ever take no for an answer; someone will say yes if you keep asking. Believe in yourself. Don't ever treat life like a rehearsal. Do what you love and if you are good at it, the money will follow. The beaten path has already been taken, so blaze a new one for yourself. Don't ever be content with what you have done; there is only one time to quit, and God lets you know when that time has come."

Introducing Jack Kalvan

Jack Kalvan is an entertainer who currently resides in Los Angeles but works all over the world. His training includes a number of comedy, acting, and dance classes, including Greg Dean's Stand-Up Comedy Workshop in Los Angeles.

Jack was born in Miami, Florida, in 1968. At the age of twelve, he unwittingly determined his fate by teaching himself to juggle three balls. Juggling quickly became his main love and obsession. Jack honed his juggling skills for many years, while fulfilling more scholarly ambitions: a degree in Mechanical Engineering from Carnegie Mellon University in Pittsburgh and then a job in robotics at IBM Research in Yorktown Heights, New York. "My job was actually building and teaching a robot to juggle," he says. Finally, he quit that job to pursue his true love, a career in juggling. Since 1989, Jack has performed as a solo act and as half of the comedy juggling team, Clockwork.

"I had so much fun practicing juggling, I spent most of my free time doing it. I was becoming pretty well known by other jugglers. When people offered me money to juggle, I could not turn it down. While I was working at IBM in New York, many of my friends were doing street shows. It looked like fun and they were making pretty good money at it. I did some of my first shows passing the hat in New York, in Central Park and Washington Square.

"Now, much of my time is spent at home. But when I do work, I make enough money to live on the rest of the time. Every couple of weeks I spend a day on the phone calling up agents and trying to get work. There are times when I work every day for long periods of time. A few years ago when I was performing at a lot of colleges, my days were mostly spent driving to the next show and sleeping in hotels. Usually I am employed for one show at a time but occasionally I get work for longer periods of time.

"Last year I spent five weeks in Atlantic City in the revue show at the Showboat. I have been to Japan four times, with a fifth trip planned for later this year. I have worked on numerous cruise ships, where most of my time is spent doing nothing. Ships get pretty boring after a while. Shortly after getting married in 1995, I was able to take my wife to Berlin for a few months while I worked at the Wintergarten. Now I won't take any long-term work unless I can take my wife with me. I now have a three-week-old daughter, so leaving is even harder.

"I am currently spending a lot of my time working on an all new show: writing new routines and rehearsing, also writing and designing all new promotional materials.

"The best thing about this career is that I get paid to juggle. And I am paid well enough that I can spend most of my time at home with my family, doing whatever I want. I don't have to get up early (usually) and I don't have to work in an office. I am self-employed and can take the shows I want and not take the shows I don't want.

"At first the travel was very exciting—getting to see the world—but now it's one of the things I like least because I usually don't have time to go sightseeing. Most of the time is spent traveling to shows and traveling home. Lugging trunks of props around can sometimes be a pain. Sleeping on airplanes is not much fun. Being away from my wife for more than a day is hard.

"I have worked with a partner, Rick Rubenstein, for many years doing a two-man show called Clockwork. We met in college, became friends and then partners. However, I am slowly making the transition to performing exclusively solo shows.

"I would advise that you not expect to become famous or wealthy. Remember that it may take years before you have a good show. Be original; the world doesn't need any more corny juggling acts. Research, but do not copy what others have done. Do what you are good at. Never be satisfied with your show; always strive for improvement."

Introducing Doubble Troubble Jugglers

Nick and Alex Karvounis are based in Las Vegas but work all over the world, including the Royal Caribbean Cruise Line.

Nick earned a bachelor of arts degree in film and television production (producing) from New York University and Alex received a bachelor arts degree in film and television production (cinematography) from New York University.

"Alex and I began juggling in the fourth grade at Pot Spring Elementary school," says Nick. "Our gym teacher, Tom Taylor, taught the entire fourth grade during class. Of the hundreds of children he taught over the years, Alex and I were the only ones to continue juggling more than just as a hobby. On weekends during middle and high school, we practiced juggling with many amateurs and professionals at the Baltimore Jugglers Club. Here we got to meet many other jugglers and professionals. By this time, Alex and I were already performing a twenty-minute magic and juggling show for children's birthday parties. We enjoyed making people laugh. I think in the long run, the reason we continue to perform our comedy/variety show is the satisfaction and joy you get when you step out onto stage and make a theater of thousands of people laugh. I remember seeing an article on Anthony Gatto, another juggler from Baltimore, and his job in Las Vegas. I remember seeing a photo of him on stage juggling seven rings. I said 'Wow!' And that's another reason I love to perform. I love to see people walk away from our show and say 'Wow . . . amazing.' Pure satisfaction!

"After performing at local children's birthday parties, local conventions, and other events in Baltimore on the weekends during high school, Alex and I went to college. Our four years at New York University in the heart of the Big Apple proved to be rewarding. It was during the summers that we worked at a resort in the Poconos. Here, we worked as camp counselors during the day and entertained at night. I remember the first time we performed onstage as an opening act for a comedian. The manager asked us to do fifteen minutes. We had no concept of time, and ran over thirty minutes. Needless to say, they still invited us back. We also began to experiment with street performing. Street performing is where an act can really become refined. It is when you are out on the street that you really learn how to keep an audience. If your show isn't interesting enough, or funny enough, or exciting enough, the audience will leave. I am truly convinced that the street is what makes or breaks an act. The street will separate the good from the bad, the strong from the weak. The street is where we learned to deal with hecklers in the crowd. This experience with street performing and passing the hat for a few bucks is where we really learned to appreciate the audience. The only reason we as entertainers survive is because the audience decides that we should survive. The second the audience stops liking you, you're dead.

"From the raw street, we moved on to theme parks. Theme parks are interesting in the fact that even though you are performing on the street, you don't have to worry about making money. You have a set salary, and whether people like you or not, you still get paid. If it rains, big deal. You still get paid. The best part of the theme parks is that you are forced to do six shows a day. Because of this, you really are forced to come up with lots of material. Our show began its true form in the theme parks. Bush Gardens Williamsburg was the first place we worked at. Here our show lasted about fifteen minutes. After an entire summer in Bush Gardens, we really got a power-packed, fifteen-minute show together. The following summer, we worked at Walt Disney World in Orlando, Florida. An agent from Disney saw us competing at a juggling convention and signed us up to work. We performed many places in Disney, including the Magic Kingdom, Pleasure Island, MGM Studios, Epcot Center, Disney's Boardwalk, and the

Marketplace. Disney has a very family-oriented style, so we had to target our show to families. After two years of Disney, our fifteen-minute show had turned into a full sixty-minute variety show.

"After relocating to Orlando for work with Disney, we were offered our first cruise ship job. Cruise ships are definitely the place to be these days. The theaters that we perform in are more beautiful than most showrooms in Las Vegas. They are state-of-the-art theaters which hold more than a thousand people and have forty-foot stage ceilings, with orchestra pits, and millions of dollars worth of lights and sets. Las Vegas used to be the place to be if you were a variety artist, but the cruise ships have taken over. Our work is exclusively with Royal Caribbean Cruise Line for one and only one reason. Professional entertainment. On a seven-day cruise with RCCL, you can expect to see two celebrity entertainers, two large-scale-production shows, and three to four other variety artists. Every act is professional and entertaining. Our work on the cruise ships is very rewarding and exciting.

"Most people look at us and say 'What an easy job you have!' They automatically think that we do our one-hour show and we are done for the week. Not so. Even though our show will last a fraction of a normal workday, there is much more that goes on behind the scenes.

"When we are between contracts and actually home in Las Vegas, much of the day is spent making phone calls and sending out promotional materials. Many phone calls are made to our agents and prospective clients searching for that next booking. This process may seem rather simple; however, most of the results may take weeks, even months, to come about. In the meantime we are busy on the computer, designing new brochures and updating materials for our portfolio. Whether it be videotape covers or a simple schedule update, all has to be designed, printed, and put together in a press package. It takes days and weeks to prepare the exact look we want for the client. With the advent of the home desktop publishing software, Alex and I have recently been designing new promotional materials directed specifically to a prospective client, adding that personal touch to the promotional material. For instance, when we were busy designing video covers for the National Basketball Association, we changed our old cover to add photos of the NBA with our pictures as well, thus making it much more personalized.

"The day continues with the unexpected as well. The phone rings and it is our agent asking if we can send out our newest promotional video immediately to a client for a last-minute job. Everything in our home office stops so that we can send out this package overnight halfway around the world. One hour later, after a long line at the post office, we are back in the office with our projects still waiting for us.

"Evening comes and we are still working. People wonder why we don't stop at five o'clock. It may be quitting time in Las Vegas but halfway around the world in Tokyo, there is an agent who needs to talk to us. We have come to find that there are no office hours in this business as well as no weekends or holidays. When the phone rings, the phone rings, and if you don't pick it up you may miss an important job. And it has happened to us before, so we quickly learned our lesson.

"When the time comes and we need our exercise, it is time to go to the gym (or more appropriately local racquetball court) to try out our new routines. Many people ask how often we put a new routine in our show. For most jugglers it takes months, if not years, to perfect a new routine with new props and choreography. It is almost impossible to simply add ten minutes of material overnight, in comparison to say a magician, who can go buy a new illusion and put it into his or her show the next week. A typical rehearsal might run an hour consisting of new material only. We don't rehearse anything in our show that has already been perfected. Doing the show over and over is practice in itself. The new material comes with trial and error. What feels right and looks right begins to take place. This process becomes quite frustrating because when you are learning new tricks you will drop things. And there is nothing like the sound of balls and clubs and knives crashing to the floor in a noisy racquetball court. All this pays off of course when the trick is perfected and applause and laughter come from the audience.

"The new comedy in our act (as with any stand-up comedian) comes from two places. First, a lot of comedy material comes by accident. When we are in the middle of our show and someone slips, says the wrong word, or sees someone in the audience to make a funny comment about, the new comedy is born. That's why we make it a point to videotape or audiotape every show we perform, otherwise you may forget what happened in the middle of the show that was so funny. Secondly, our comedy comes when we are surrounded by friends, possibly late at night in a hot tub, when we are just sitting around throwing ideas about. This occurs sporadically throughout the week, sometimes more often, sometimes less often.

"The night is drawing close to an end and all we have left to do is discuss what has to been done tomorrow. We close up shop for the night and check out the comics on late night television.

"The most rewarding part of the job is the actual show. That is by far the most exciting; seeing and hearing an audience laugh and respond to the juggling and comedy. The travel also makes for a very unique and interesting part of the job. We are in a position to do what we love to do and see parts of the world we thought we'd only see in history books or on the Travel Channel. Our performing has taken us to nearly every continent on the earth and seeing and meeting people of every culture and background. It has been a learning experience far beyond anything we could have expected, which is what makes us enjoy taking our show on the road.

"The only drawback may seem rather minor, but when you travel forty-five weeks a year it really begins to eat you alive. Most annoying is the actual travel to each gig. Many times you are waiting in a crowded airport for hours for your flight. Whether it be from weather delays or overbookings, something always comes up that delays your flight and travel plans. I'd say that the flying becomes the most frustrating event of the entire business (first class helps alleviate this problem slightly, if you are fortunate enough to get first class). It is this part of the day that begins to wear on you physically, lugging your travel cases and luggage from one terminal to another, from one shuttle bus to another, and finally to the hotel. These are minor problems on the outside but again when you are doing this six days a week it becomes very tedious. There is an upside to this problem with airports, though. We can tell you where any men's room is at most airports around the world, as well as restaurants, cafés, and business centers, and which airports have free luggage carts, and which airports have VW Bugs for taxis.

"There is more to performing than just knowing how to juggle. There have been some great jugglers in the past who couldn't entertain an audience. The novelty of juggling wears off quickly so you must come up with something unique to keep the audience's interest. To keep your show interesting, you must make the audience like and relate to you onstage. Finally, the most important thing is that you have to enjoy what you are doing. If not, move on and try something else. Good luck!"

Introducing Jonathon Wee

Jonathon Wee is a San Francisco-based entertainer. He has a bachelor of arts degree in economics from Luther College, a small private liberal arts college in Iowa.

"I am mostly self-taught," he says. "I learned a lot from going to juggling festivals and seeing other jugglers and juggling with them. Jugglers are very generous about teaching one another.

"I've been known by the following titles: Professional Juggler, Juggler/Comedian, Performing Juggler, or Luckiest Man on Earth. And more specifically, I am one member of a two-person comedy juggling team, or duo, and we are called the Passing Zone.

"I learned to juggle three bean bags when I was in eighth grade at the age of thirteen," he says. "A woman was teaching a few people to juggle and I thought it looked like fun, so I joined in and was immediately hooked. I would spend much of my spare time just standing in a corner of the room, or outside, or wherever I could find space, and juggling for hours. Then I taught two friends, and the three of us started doing little shows for birthday parties, picnics, things like that. Our first real job of any distinction was at the Minnesota Renaissance Festival at age fifteen.

"I was first fascinated with the juggling itself. The feeling of satisfaction of learning something that seemed impossible, but soon became easier and easier, was compelling. And there were no boundaries—just so many possibilities. Hundreds of tricks with three balls, then working on four balls, then tricks with four, then five, etc. And then when that got boring all I had to do was pick up rings or clubs (the things that look like bowling pins) or flaming torches, and it was all new again. And it was a fun thing to do with others. Either to teach each other, show off what we had learned, or challenge the other person or people to do what you can do. Next step was cooperating and learning to pass between two or three or more people. That group effort and accomplishment was a fun way to meet and bond with people. But I became truly attracted to it as a profession when I got onstage and realized that I could make people laugh and applaud. And the fact that I could actually get paid for it was almost too good to be true! I still think that nearly every day, and I've been performing for about seventeen years.

"One summer during college, I had a job laying sod. It was the most miserable working experience I had ever had. It was dirty, back-breaking, horrible work with the most disagreeable people I had had the pleasure of knowing. It was then that I knew that juggling was something really wonderful. I enjoyed it so much and the pay was decidedly better. I still had some thoughts about a real job after college, but I knew my college education was at least going to keep me out of doing hard labor, and I was glad about that.

"I had some experience acting and singing, and I think that added to my comfort level and enjoyment of being onstage in front of people. All my life, I can remember receiving profound satisfaction from making people laugh.

"A typical day at home (at the home office) is get up at 9:30, have some breakfast, make whatever phone calls are most urgent from the previous day, or that have come in before I get to my answering machine. These usually include calls to agents or clients to discuss details of upcoming shows, or perhaps flight arrangements, or talk with people who have heard of our show and want promotional materials. Then I take my dog and laptop computer for a walk to my neighborhood coffee shop, where I sit and either work on writing new comedy and juggling routines or on script ideas for upcoming shows. We often customize our performances to fit a corporate client's needs by juggling their products, making jokes or references to their industry or company, etc. I might also work on memorizing scripts for upcoming shows or a variety of assorted office tasks.

"Then I go home and spend most of the afternoon working at my desk. There are lots of phone calls, both coming in and going out. There is much to attend to—printing and sending contracts and invoices, travel and hotel arrangements. Then on a good day (but too rare) I will go to the gym and practice juggling for an hour or two. Then I go for a run, get back to the house when my wife is getting home from work, and we spend the evening together. Then after she goes to bed, I often spend a couple of hours doing more work in my office (like now), or maybe practice guitar, or watch Letterman and Conan, or all of the above.

"On a performance day, I get up at 6 or 7 A.M., dash to the airport, fly to Chicago or Atlanta or Dallas or Miami, or virtually anywhere in the country. We are usually picked up at the airport and brought to our hotel by about 4 or 5 P.M. Often, in the corporate market, we are performing in the hotel ballroom or other special event space, which is very convenient. We set up and do a sound check for about an hour, then grab a quick bite to eat, sometimes with a client, sometimes not, go back to my room to iron clothes and change for the performance. The show often is at 8 or 9 P.M., and we usually perform anywhere from thirty to sixty minutes (often forty-five), depending what the client wants.

Then we take an hour to pack up, get back to our room, maybe order room service, watch Letterman and Conan, and go to sleep. The next day we catch a 10 A.M. flight back home, or on to the next city to repeat the process.

"That's the most common day, but we also work comedy clubs, cruise ships, NBA half-time shows, and other venues that are very different and require very different schedules.

"Mostly, we work evenings and weekends, although there is plenty of work during the week as well.

"I love making people laugh. I love being able to travel and meet interesting people in exotic and fun places. Often we are working at what is someone else's vacation spot, or at least it is at an event at which people are supposed to be having fun. So often it's good food, nice hotels, big cities, or gorgeous beaches. I love the incredible satisfaction and joy of a standing ovation, of getting that kind of immediate feedback and having people come up to me afterward and say how much they enjoyed it. And it is a non-stop creative outlet, writing new material, trying new jokes, imagining what I want to be doing in the future and working toward that goal. And I love the possibilities. I never know what the next phone call is going to be, and it could be a great new gig, a trip around the world, a spot on a television show, or it could be an audition for our own television show or movie—anything! If my career stayed where it is now I would be happy, but knowing that I could someday be famous and making millions makes it constantly exciting. And I love being self-employed and making my own schedule.

"My least favorite thing is the travel. Or not so much the travel but the need to be away from home so much, and away from my wife. And, while I like the flexibility of my job, sometimes the lack of a routine and the uncertainty of where the next checks are going to come from can leave me feeling very frazzled and detached from what can be called a 'normal' life. Sometimes it would just be nice to be home for a month, or even a week! The travel really is the only downside, and since some aspects of travel actually fit into the upside category, it is a downside I can certainly live with.

"I would advise that you practice hard and perform whenever you can. The only way to learn how to be a performer is to get up in front of people and perform. Be original. Follow your heart. And expect that it may take a long time to be able to make it work well, but it is worth the wait and the effort. It's the best job in the world!"

Introducing the Nocks

The Nocks are a family of performers who engage in a variety of acts all over the world. They have been appearing at the Tommy Bartlett Show at the Wisconsin Dells for the past nineteen years. A special honor includes the family's recent induction into the Circle of Fame, a Sarasota, Florida, organization which recognizes circus greats.

Eugene Nocks Jr. reports that "everybody in my generation has followed into this profession. There are four sons, the youngest of whom is twenty-five. The next generation includes my three sons, my brother's daughter and a son, and my other brother's daughter. Even though they're still school age, some have started to experience the thrill of working in the circus.

"I began practicing as a performer when I was seven," says Nocks. "I started doing what we call the swaypole, which looks like a flagpole. You climb to the top with your feet in your hands. Once you master the technique, you are, in effect, walking up the pole. It's about eighty feet in a matter of about forty-five seconds. At the age of fourteen, I had perfected the routine and began performing.

"My brother John, who is the second oldest, started working on his act, the pyramid of chairs, at the age of eight. He is what we call an *equilibrist* (a balancer). He can do handstands on chairs up to as many as six at one time. In other words, he makes a pyramid of all of these chairs and then balances on top of them. This was so unusual for such a young person to accomplish that he became very famous when he was very young. He was asked to perform on many television shows including the Bozo show (about eight times) and other shows around the world.

"Our third oldest brother, Michael Angelo, was always into trapezes. He started when he was an early teenager, doing front and back levers and handstands. He perfected two tricks that I believe only two or three people in the world are capable of doing. The first is called a one-arm back flange and the other trick is a handstand on the trapeze completely free. Michael Angelo was about eleven when he was an actor in the show *Peter Pan*, starring Cathy Rigby. Actually we all worked on that show. My three brothers were the Darling children and I was one of the pirates. We were picked because we were very comfortable with flying.

"Our youngest brother, Bello, who started working on his act at the age of six, is presently in Mexico City doing a show for Televisa, which is an international television station over there. He's rapidly becoming a very famous clown because he has such a knack for entertainment. He makes you laugh just by walking into the room with his funny faces and other antics. He's traveling around the world doing one-man shows.

"Because of invitations to appear and perform, we have always traveled a lot—Australia, New Zealand, the Far East, and, of course, all of America and Canada. I personally have been around the world four times. My mother has traveled around the world countless times and, as a result, speaks seven languages.

"We have been asked to perform in a number of unusual circumstances. For instance, in 1994, the Wisconsin Film Commission called us to help them with a Powerball commercial they wanted to film. The idea was to put together an amazing feat with one human catcher who would receive up to six humans at one time. With seven balls in the lottery, the one Powerball person would be dressed in red and the rest of us in white leotards with numbers on the front and back. It took us three days to film this incredible stunt.

"We've also been hired to do a number of performances at various car races. The stock car people particularly seem to like what we do. Appearances include Daytona and the Charlotte Motor Speedway.

"The Philadelphia Phillies have always liked us, too. We've done many baseball drops or baseball first pitches using unusual circumstances. For instance, one year my brother Michael was suspended from a helicopter. Another time one of us threw the first pitch from the ninety-foot swaypole.

"Our family has been presenting this type of entertainment since, believe it or not, 1840. Back then, it might have been a promotional event like the opening of a new department store, or something of that nature. They would set up a wire from one side of the street to the other, for instance, and one of the Nocks would walk across and be the first customer.

"If we are not performing, we are perfecting our routines. Thousands of hours are spent in bringing these acts to the point where they are safe and we feel comfortable with them. When we are not doing that, we are working on developing new acts. For instance, at Sea World in Texas, we presented a thirty-minute show called "Wheels." Everything in the show, which was performed six times per day, was on wheels—skateboards, unicycles, bicycles, motorcycles, go-carts, all kinds of wheels. So we're always thinking about new ideas which can provide the concept for a new show. When we're not working on that, we may be doing bookkeeping, sound work, or maintenance of the equipment.

"There are other things that will be a measure of whether on not you will be successful in this field. For instance, it's important for people in the entertainment business to have the right attitude, a very aggressive outlook on life, since they must be comfortable with large groups and be able to conduct interviews and so on. We usually travel with a group of about one hundred people, so you also have to know how to get along with others in close quarters. In addition, you have to stay in shape year-round, exercising, doing daily push-ups, chin-ups, and sit-ups. And you have to maintain your health and control your diet. Especially in third world countries you must be careful, because your diet could affect your performance.

"This is a most interesting business. Performing is very magical and being able to do it with other members of your family makes it even more special. All of us are in it for keeps. My seventy-two-year-old uncle, who is a professional clown/slapstick comedian, still performs his craft, mostly in Europe. He hasn't even thought of retiring yet—in fact no one in the family has!"

Here is your next birth name challenge:
Melvin Kaminsky

For More Information

Cahners Business Newspapers
5700 Wilshire Boulevard, Suite 120
Los Angeles, CA 90036

Daily Variety. 5700 Wilshire Boulevard, Suite 120, Los Angeles, CA 90036. Daily tabloid for the entertainment industry.

Screen Actors Guild
7065 Hollywood Boulevard
Hollywood, CA 90028

Screen Actors Guild
1515 Broadway
New York, NY 10036

CHAPTER FIVE

Magicians

"Live merrily as thou canst, for by honest mirth we cure many passions of the mind." ROBERT BURTON

D o you know who this is describing?

1. Birth name—David Seth Kotkin

2. Birth date—September 16, 1956

3. Gave his first magic show at the age of ten

4. The youngest-ever member of the Society of American Magicians at twelve

5. Before leaving high school, he taught a few classes of magic to drama students at New York University

6. First performance on Broadway was in *The Magic Man*

7. Worth about $85 million as of 1996

If you guessed David Copperfield, you'd be right! Of course, not everyone will be as successful as David Copperfield, but many are content to enjoy a measure of success as professional magicians.

Zeroing in on What a Magician Does

Magicians perform original and stock tricks of illusion and sleight of hand, using their creative powers and a variety of props to entertain and mystify an audience. Magicians are masters of illusion. They do one thing, while an audience sees another. Through a combination of complicated techniques and persuasive comments, a magician can appear to pull a rabbit out of a hat, make a handkerchief disappear, or perform a wide variety of other tricks.

A magician may include a participant from the audience and secretly remove the participant's wallet from his or her pocket while a delighted audience looks on. Or a magician may use a wooden box or other prop to appear to saw a trained assistant in half. Magicians generally use props such as illusion boxes, cards, or coins. Although many magicians perform similar tricks, each magician brings a unique style to his or her performance. It takes a high degree of skill to perform the different illusions. The more skilled and experienced the magician, the more complicated the illusions.

On the Job as a Magician

Generally, magicians work indoors in front of audiences. They may perform in front of large crowds at a theater, for example, or for just a few people at a birthday party. Magicians often work alone, but it is not unusual for a magician to have one or two assistants help at a performance. At times, a magician may have to move heavy props, such as tables or large boxes.

The Road to Magic

Magicians are skilled entertainers. It can take years of practice and training to become an accomplished magician, yet it is often possible to learn some of the more basic tricks in just a short time.

Professional magicians rarely reveal in public how they performed their tricks. The reasons are obvious. If everyone knows how a trick is done, it is no longer a trick. The element of surprise and wonder would be gone. For this reason, the most common form of training is for a budding magician to study under a professional magician. In this way, neophyte magicians learn how to perform the various illusions. Many beginning magicians start their careers as assistants for more experienced magicians.

Talk to several magicians who live in your area to find out how they feel about their work. It's also worthwhile to read books that explain some of the basic magic tricks. Try performing them in front of your family and friends. Then prepare a performance for a school or other group and see how you feel about doing this on a regular basis.

People generally do not take college or high school courses to learn magic tricks, although courses in acting or public speaking can help a magician become more effective. It is important for a magician to have good business skills, since magicians usually handle their own financial matters. It is also important for magicians to have strong sales skills since they are always, in effect, selling themselves and their abilities to prospective clients.

A good magician is an actor who is able to deceive people without making them feel silly or embarrassed. It is important for a magician to be comfortable performing in front of large groups of people and to be creative in developing original forms of presentation.

Dollars and Sense

While world-famous magicians such as Doug Henning and David Copperfield can earn many thousands of dollars for each performance, most magicians do not earn enough from their performances to support themselves financially. The vast majority of magicians are those who perform nights or on weekends and have other full- or part-time jobs. A magician may earn anywhere from fifty dollars for performing at a birthday party to several thousand dollars for performing at a business meeting or magic show.

Like other performance artists, magicians face an uncertain employment picture. Highly skilled magicians should find many job opportunities, while those just beginning may find it difficult to secure employment. There has been a trend for some businesses to hire magicians at trade shows and sales meetings to improve interest in a product. This should create some well-paying opportunities for those with the skill and a good reputation.

Words from the Pros

Introducing Carl Andrews Jr.

Carl Andrews Jr. is a comedy sleight-of-hand expert who lives and works in Hawaii. Playing the guitar in high school bands was his official introduction to show business, and he credits his success with magic to years and years of practicing his craft and "by reading every book I could get my hands on about magic." He feels that his fascination with magic is something that everyone experiences at one time or another. One of the mottoes he lives by is: "If you're not living on the edge, you're taking up too much space."

"My routine consists of doing my phone work and E-mail in the morning and taking care of any mailings that need to go out," he explains. "Then I rehearse new routines and do some reading or studying videotapes in the afternoon. In the evening I perform, then come home and answer more E-mail.

"What I like most is working for myself and doing what I enjoy for a living—which is making people laugh. I love to entertain. The only downsides would be when business is slow and being self-employed means no paid vacations.

"I would advise everyone to study and read all you can about the field and the art of magic. Develop your own unique performing character and style. Then practice, practice, practice!"

Introducing Bill Palmer

Bill Palmer earned a bachelor of arts degree in Germanics from Rice University in Houston and also studied music at the University of Houston for three years, but he credits his success as a magician to on-the-job training and "plenty of seminars." He comes from a family of entertainers; his father was a music educator and concert artist, so he got started when he was just a child. He saw Harry Blackstone Sr. perform his vanishing bird cage trick in a live show, and said to himself, "That's what I want to do when I grow up!" Besides performing his magic shows, he has also played in several bands.

"I work from my home, so my day is what I make it. My work is seasonal, so during the off-season, I have to find alternate ways to occupy my time so I write and build magic props and banjos.

"I like the accolades I receive when I do a good show; I'm an applause junkie. But I dislike the grunt work—packing and setting up. The upside of being a magician is that there are people I have entertained for three generations now. But the downside is the same—there are people I have entertained for three generations now!

"To anyone wanting to follow in my footsteps, I would like to say, 'Wear boots; it gets deep!' Actually, I would say don't take up entertaining unless you are willing to learn your craft from the ground up. Learn the fundamentals, then expand on them. Study with the best. Take drama courses. Learn to read and speak well. Be yourself. And take vitamins!"

Introducing Larry Moss

From his home in Rochester, New York, Larry Moss runs an entertainment business called Fooled Ya. He earned both a bachelor of arts degree in math–computer science and a master of science in elementary education from the University of Rochester, but says he has no formal training in the three things he teaches and performs now—magic, juggling, and balloon art. He also wrote a book on balloon sculpting that is distributed all over the world, and he maintains a Web site on the Internet that offers a collection of resources for balloon artists.

"My background is in music," he explains. "I started playing the violin at five years old and continued through high school. I had intended to further pursue music, but I got sidetracked when putting together a wizard costume for Halloween one year. Being a performer, I went a little overboard learning to play the part of a wizard, and I discovered that magic was a wide-open field for creative expression that I enjoyed even more than playing the violin.

"It was actually an accident that I ended up going into entertaining full-time. Making people laugh has always been a big part of who I am and what I do, but it wasn't something I expected to do for a living. I paid my way through college by performing on street corners and at birthday parties. I got my bachelor of arts degree, took a real job, then decided I wasn't happy. So I went back to school and again paid for my education by performing. It was only when I finished school the second time that I realized what I enjoyed most was entertaining. Most importantly, having paid my way through school—twice—by performing, I knew it could work.

"I watch all the performers I can, all the time. I don't care if they're in my field or not. I've been influenced heavily by people doing things as diverse as clowning or ballet. I don't have a 'typical' day. I suppose the largest portion of my time is spent being a salesman. I sell myself and my art all day long, everywhere I go. It's not an imposing sort of selling. Mostly, I'm just being myself. I'm always 'on' and always ready to talk about my business if the opportunity arises.

"Outside of that, my time gets divided into writing about what I do, rehearsing for shows, creating new routines, and simply playing with balloons. When I'm feeling most stressed out, I simply take out balloons and just play. Of course, playing with balloons amounts to practicing and being creative. So, in a sense, I don't ever take a vacation from my work. On the other hand, I don't need one. I'm just enjoying myself when I do work.

"The best part about this kind of work is that I rarely see people who aren't happy. If they aren't in a great mood when I arrive, they almost always are when I leave. I get paid to make people happy. What could be more fun than that?

"The worst part is that I tend to be working when my friends aren't—because I'm performing at the parties that everyone else is throwing. Another negative is that work, and therefore income, can be very inconsistent. I can have a few great weeks and then a few poor ones. I can never predict what work I'll have at any given time.

"An entertainer makes a career by being different from others. Everyone looking to get into entertainment has to find their own differences and work on those above all else. Classical training can only go so far. If you only have the same skills as others around you, you can easily be replaced. But if you're unique, you'll always be needed by someone."

Here is your next birth name challenge:
Nathan Birnbaum

For More Information

The International Brotherhood of Magicians (IBM), founded in 1922, is the world's largest organization for magicians. The organization boasts a membership of over fourteen thousand members worldwide. There are over three hundred regional organizations called Rings in more than seventy-three countries. The International Brotherhood of Magicians is a respected organization for amateur as well as professional magicians. IBM's Web site is http://www.magician.org/.

The Society of American Magicians (SAM) was formed in 1902 and is the oldest active organization for magic in the world. It has seventy-five hundred members. There are chapters in England, Hong Kong, Japan, and Germany. SAM's monthly magazine is called *mum*. SAM actively promotes magic as an entertainment and art form and has the world's largest youth program for magic called the Society for Young Magicians (SYM) with fourteen hundred members. Youths between the ages of seven and fifteen may join SYM. SYM's E-mail address is rmBlowers@aol.com.

In addition, you can write to:

Magical Youth International
61551 Bremen Highway
Mishawaka, IN 46544

Society of American Magicians
P. O. Box 290068
St. Louis, MO 63129

CHAPTER SIX

Performers

"The most wasted day of all is that on which we have not laughed."
NICOLAS CHAMFORT

F or some who are class clowns at heart, performing takes the form of singing or acting. Are music and performing at the core of your very being, something from which you derive great enjoyment? Has music always been a special part of your life? Are you one of the people who has always longed to appear before audiences? Did you ever stand in front of your mirror and pretend your hairbrush was a microphone? Did you play your musical instruments for friends, family, pets—virtually anyone who would listen?

For the Musically Inclined

Successful professional musicians are artists who express themselves through their music by conducting, playing instruments or singing (or both). Through their talent, many years of hard work, initiative, and perhaps a lucky break, they make a living and entertain audiences doing what they love most, making music.

Some musically inclined individuals succeed early in life—Lorin Maazel conducted two major symphony orchestras before the age of thirteen and went on to enjoy a successful career as an adult conductor. Yehudi Menuhin made his violin debut at seven. Sergei Prokofiev was already performing as a pianist at the ripe old age of six and composed an opera at the age of nine. His *Peter and the Wolf* has been a source of entertainment for both children and adults for many decades.

No matter how old you are, the following chapter will provide you with the information you need to pursue a career in performing music.

Musicians

The number of musicians who perform in the United States is estimated to be about 256,000. Included are those who play in any one of thirty-nine regional, ninety metropolitan, or thirty major symphony orchestras. (Large orchestras employ from 85 to 105 musicians while smaller ones employ 60 to 75 players.) Also counted are those who are a part of hundreds of small orchestras, symphony orchestras, pop and jazz groups, and those who broadcast or record.

Instrumental musicians may play a variety of musical instruments in an orchestra, popular band, marching band, military band, concert band, symphony, dance band, rock group, or jazz group and may specialize in string, brass, woodwind, percussion instruments, or electronic synthesizers. A large percentage of musicians are proficient in playing several related instruments, such as the flute and clarinet. Those who are very talented have the option to perform as soloists.

Rehearsing and performing take up much of the musicians' time and energy. In addition, musicians, especially those without agents, may need to perform a number of other routine tasks such as making reservations; keeping track of auditions and/or recordings; arranging for sound effects amplifiers and other equipment to enhance performances; designing lighting, costuming, and makeup; bookkeeping; and setting up advertising, concerts, tickets, programs, and contracts. In addition, it is necessary for musicians to plan the sequence of the numbers to be performed and/or arrange their music according to the conductor's instructions before performances.

Musicians must also keep their instruments clean, polished, tuned, and in proper working order. In addition, they are expected to attend meetings with agents, employers, and conductors or directors to discuss contracts, engagements, and any other business activities.

Performing musicians encompass a wide variety of careers. Just a few of the possibilities are described on the following pages.

Session Musician

The session musician is the one responsible for playing background music in a studio while a recording artist is singing. The session musician may also be called a freelance musician, a backup musician, a session player, or studio musician. Session musicians are used for all kinds of recordings, Broadway musicals, operas, rock and folk songs, and pop tunes.

Versatility is the most important ingredient for these professionals—the more instruments the musician has mastered, the greater number of styles he or she can offer, the more possibilities for musical assignments. Session musicians often are listed through contractors who call upon them when the need arises. Other possibilities exist through direct requests made by the artists themselves, the group members, or the management team.

The ability to sight-read is important for all musicians but it is particularly crucial for session musicians. Rehearsal time is usually very limited and costs make it too expensive to have to do retakes.

Section Member

Section members are the individuals who play instruments in an orchestra. They must be talented at playing their instrument of choice and able to learn the music on their own. Rehearsals are strictly designed for putting all of the instruments and individuals together, and for establishing cues such as phrasing and correct breathing. It is expected that all musicians practice sufficiently on their own before rehearsals.

Concertmaster

Those chosen to be concertmasters have the important responsibility of leading the string sections of the orchestras during both rehearsals and concerts. In addition, these individuals are responsible for tuning the rest of the orchestra. This is the "music" you hear for about fifteen to twenty seconds before the musicians begin to play their first piece.

Concertmasters answer directly to the conductor. They must possess leadership abilities and be very knowledgeable of both the music and all the instruments.

Floor Show Band Member

Musicians who belong to bands that perform floor shows appear in hotels, nightclubs, cruise ships, bars, concert arenas, and cafés. Usually the bands do two shows per night with a particular number of sets in each show. Additionally, they may be required to play one or two dance sets during the course of the engagement. The audience is seated during the shows and gets up to dance during the dance sets. Shows may include costuming, dialogue, singing, jokes, skits, unusual sound effects, and anything else the band decides to include. Floor show bands may be contracted to appear in one place for one night or several weeks at a time. As expected, a lot of traveling is involved for those who take up this career.

Church or Temple Choir Director

Choir directors are responsible for recruiting and directing choirs and planning the music programs. They are often given the job of auditioning potential members of the choir, setting up rehearsal schedules, overseeing and directing rehearsals, and choosing the music. They may be in charge of the church's or temple's music library or may designate another individual to oversee it. Working closely with the minister or other religious leader of the congregation, choir directors plan all concerts, programs, and other musical events.

In addition, choir directors develop and maintain the music budgets for their religious institutions. In some cases, choral directors are expected to maintain office hours each week. During those times, individuals may write music, handle administrative chores, or work with small groups of singers and/or the organist.

Usually a bachelor's degree in church music is required; often a master's degree is requested.

Organist

Organists play their instruments at religious and special services like weddings and funerals. Recitals may also be given as part of the congregation's spiritual programming. Organists choose the music to be played or may work with the choir or music director to accomplish this task. Organists are also responsible for making sure organs are in proper working order and may also advise the congregation on other music-related issues. Sometimes the organist is also the choir director.

Singer

Singers use their voices as their instruments of choice. Using the techniques of melody, harmony, rhythm, and voice production, they interpret music and both instruct and entertain their audiences. They may sing character parts or perform in their own individual style.

Classical singers are identified by the ranges of their voices: soprano (highest range), contralto, tenor, baritone, and bass (lowest range). These singers will typically perform in operas.

Singers of popular music may perform country and western, ethnic, reggae, folk, rock, or jazz as individuals or as part of a group. Often singers also possess the ability to play musical instruments and thus accompany themselves when performing (guitar or piano, for instance).

Religious singers include cantors, soloists, or choral members.

Announcer/Disc Jockey

Announcers play an important role in keeping listeners tuned into a radio or television station. They are the ones who must read messages, commercials, and scripts in an entertaining, interesting, and/or enlightening way. They are also responsible for introducing station breaks, and they may interview guests and sell commercial time to advertisers. Sometimes they are called disc jockeys, but actually disc jockeys are the announcers who oversee musical programming.

Disc jockeys must be very knowledgeable about music in general and all aspects of their specialties, specifically the music and the groups who play and/or sing that kind of music. Their programs may feature general music, rock, pop, country and western, or any specific musical period or style such as 1950s or 1960s tunes.

Conductor and Choral Director

The music conductor is the director for all of the performers in a musical presentation, whether it be singing or instrumental. Though there are many types of conductors—symphony, choral, dance band, opera, marching band, and ballet—in all cases the music conductor is the one who is in charge of interpreting the music.

Conductors audition and select musicians, choose the music to accommodate the talents and abilities of the musicians, and direct rehearsals and performances, applying conducting techniques to achieve desired musical effects like harmony, rhythm, tempo, and shading.

Orchestral conductors lead instrumental music groups, such as orchestras, dance bands, and various popular ensembles. Choral directors lead choirs and glee clubs, sometimes working with a band or orchestra conductor.

Where the Musicians Roam

Popular instrumentalists are spread nationwide from small towns to large cities. Many consist of small groups that play at weddings, Bar Mitzvahs, church events, funerals, school or community concerts, dances, festivals, and other events. Accompanists play for theatre productions or dance recitals. Combos, piano or organ soloists, and other musicians play at nightclubs, bars, or restaurants. Musicians may work in opera, musical comedy, and ballet productions or be a part of the armed forces. Well-known musicians and groups give their own concerts, appear "live" on radio and television, make recordings, movies, and music videos, or go on concert tours.

Many musicians work in cities in which there are fairly large populations and where entertainment and recording activities are concentrated, such as New York, Los Angeles, Nashville, San Francisco, Boston, Philadelphia, and Chicago.

Working Conditions for Musicians

Musicians, singers, and conductors are often forced into work schedules that are long and erratic, depending on how heavy the rehearsal and presentation schedules are. Usually daily practices or rehearsals are required, particularly for new projects. Work weeks in excess of forty hours are common. Travel is often a familiar part of a musician's or singer's life and a routine that includes daytime, nighttime, weekend, or holiday work is entirely possible.

Musicians who are lucky enough to be hired for a full season (a "master agreement") work for up to fifty-two weeks. Those who must work for more than one employer are always on the lookout for additional gigs and many supplement their incomes by finding work in other related or unrelated jobs.

Most instrumental musicians come into contact with a variety of other people, including their colleagues, agents, employers, sponsors, and audiences. They usually work indoors, although some may perform outdoors for parades, concerts, and dances. In some taverns and restaurants, smoke and odors may be present, and lighting and ventilation may be inadequate.

The Road to Music

Many people who become professional musicians begin studying their instrument of choice (whether it be voice, organ, harp, harpsichord, any string, woodwind, brass, or percussion) in childhood and continue the study via private or group lessons throughout elementary and high school. In addition, they usually garner valuable experience by playing in a school or community band or orchestra, or with a group of friends.

Singers usually start training when their voices mature. All musicians need extensive and prolonged training to acquire the necessary skills, knowledge, and ability to interpret music. Participation in school musicals, religious institutions, community events, state fairs, in a band, or in a choir often provides good early training and experience. Necessary formal training may be obtained through conservatory, college or university study, or personal study with a professional (or both).

Over six hundred colleges, universities, and conservatories offer four-year programs that result in a bachelor's degree in music education. Usually both pop and classical music are studied. Course work will include classes in music theory, music composition, music interpretation, literature, conducting, drama, foreign languages, acting, and how to play a musical instrument. Other academic studies include course work in science, literature, philosophy, and the arts. Classroom instruction, discussion groups, reading assignments, and actual performances are included. A large number of performances are encouraged and expected and students are evaluated on their progress during their time at the college.

At the undergraduate level, a typical program for a violin major might consist of the following courses:

Instrument

Materials and literature

Ear training

Piano class

Music history

Orchestra

Piano and strings chamber music

String quartet

Introduction to literature

Foreign language

Academic electives

Young persons who are considering careers in music need to have musical talent, improvisational skills, versatility, creative ability, the ability to sight-read, outstanding music memory, finger dexterity, ability to distinguish differences in pitch, determination, imagination, creativity, perseverance, ability to work with others, and poise and stage presence. Since quality performance requires constant study and practice, self-discipline is vital.

Moreover, musicians who play concert and nightclub engagements must have physical stamina because frequent travel and night performances are required. They must also be prepared to face the anxiety of intermittent employment and rejections when auditioning for work.

For announcers and disc jockeys, additional education beyond secondary school, particularly course work in public speaking, writing, English, communications, music, radio and television broadcasting, and videotape production is very advantageous. Desirable personal qualities include charisma, a pleasing voice, good timing, a good sense of humor, and expertise about the field of music. In addition, gaining experience as a production assistant or writer is beneficial, in addition to securing a radio telephone operator permit from the Federal Communications Commission (FCC).

Musical conductors must have at least a high school diploma and knowledge of the arts, musical history, harmony, and theory, along with various languages (especially French, German, Latin, and Italian). Desirable qualities include charisma, a great ear for music, an air of style, both business and musical savvy, knowledge of all instruments—particularly piano, advanced sight-reading skills, a sense of showmanship, the ability to lead, skills in performing in an appealing way, and the ability to use a baton to control timing, rhythm, and structure. Individuals become musical conductors after spending many years as musicians while, at the same time, studying to become conductors.

Financial Rewards for Musicians

Earnings in the world of music performing will depend heavily on a number of factors: experience, training, the specific instrument played, reputation, location, and whether or not you belong to a union. Bear in mind that salaries must cover expenses, travel, publicity costs, and agent or manager fees. Royalty figures average about 10 to 12 percent—escalating all the way up to 25 percent if you are a top entertainer.

Musicians are covered by the American Federation of Musicians videotape agreement guaranteeing a minimum two-hour call with payment of $55.15 per hour. Varying pay scales exist for basic cable television and documentary films.

Sample Earnings for Musicians

Symphony Orchestra Performers

Metropolitan—$35 to $85 per concert in addition to $25 to $50 per rehearsal

Regional—$400 to $700 per week (average thirty-week year, may extend to fifty-two weeks)

Major—$1,000 to $1,400 per week ($50,000 to $60,000 per year for forty-eight to fifty-two working weeks)

Soloist—$60,000 to $70,000 per year

Broadway musical—$600 to $1,000 per week for twenty working hours

Freelance musician—$40 per two-and-a-half-hour rehearsal

Freelance (union) musician—$85 per performance

Nightclub Performers

Jazz musician—$100 to $300 per night

Jazz group—$2,000 to $3,000 per week at a well-established nightclub

Recording Musicians

Studio musician—$175 to $250 for a three-hour session plus $50 for each additional thirty minutes

Motion picture recording—$200 to $260 per week depending on size of ensemble

Sound or music editor—$1,400 per week

Popular musicians may be paid for a single performance or for a number of engagements. The pay could range anywhere from $30 per performance to $300 per performance. Jazz musicians in popular clubs in New York City earn $100 to $300 per night while musicians in a Broadway musical orchestra could receive more than $600 a week for twenty hours of work.

When available, studio recording pays well—more than $175 for a three-hour session.

Sample Earnings for Vocal Performers

Earnings for singers will vary considerably depending upon the location, your experience, and the magnitude of the event.

Television and Radio

Though earnings for announcers and disc jockeys will vary according the experience, area of the country, and size of the market, salaries tend to be higher in television stations. Salaries for announcers in a small station start at $22,000 per year. A larger station would probably offer about $45,000 per year.

Groups of three to eight—$478 on camera; $288 off camera

Groups of nine or more—$417 on camera

Radio dealer commercials for a six-month period (Dealer commercials are made for a designated manufacturer for delivery to and use by its local dealers. A dealer contracts station time and is limited to using the recording as a wild spot or local program commercial.)

Actor, Announcer—$606.20

Solo or Duo—$480.85

Groups of three to five—$313.50

Groups of six to eight—$250.85

Groups of nine or more—$156.75

(*Source*: SAG/AFTRA)

Sound Effects
Performer—$158.55

(*Source:* AFTRA)

Opera
Singer in a leading role—$650 minimum per week

Solo bits—$541 per week (plus diem for a maximum of six weeks)

Well-known singer—$2,000 to $4,000 at small houses

Choral members—$950 to $1,100 per week at the Metropolitan Opera in New York

Star performers—$12,000 per performance at the Metropolitan Opera in New York

. (*Source:* Most salaries set by the American Guild of Musical Artists—AGMA)

Sample Earnings for Conductors
Conductors often negotiate on a one-to-one basis with individual orchestras to determine a salary. The size of the orchestra and the

geographic region will be factors in determining salary levels for conductors.

Part-time church choir directors—$3,500 to $25,000 per year

Full-time church choir directors—$15,000 to $40,000

Dance band—$300 to $1,200 per week

Full-time opera conductor (established)—$100,000 per year

Regional conductor—$25,000 to $40,000

International conductor—$500,000

Since they may not work steadily for one employer, some performers may not qualify for unemployment compensation, and few have either sick leave or vacations with pay. For these reasons, many musicians give private lessons or take jobs unrelated to music in order to supplement their earnings as performers.

Many musicians belong to a local of the American Federation of Musicians. Professional singers usually belong to a branch of the Associated Actors and Artists of America.

What the Future Holds for Musicians

Competition for musician jobs is keen, and talent alone is no guarantee of success. The glamour and potential high earnings in this occupation attracts many talented individuals.

The *Occupational Outlook Handbook* reports that overall employment of musicians is expected to grow faster than the average for all occupations through the year 2005. Almost all new wage and salary jobs for musicians will arise in religious organizations and in bands, orchestras, and other entertainment groups. A decline in employment is projected for salaried musicians in restaurants and bars, although they comprise a very small proportion of the total number of musicians who are salaried.

Competition is always great for announcers/disc jockeys. They must often work on a freelance rather than a salaried basis. The growth in the areas of licensing of new radio and television stations and cable television indicates an increase in the number of jobs that will be available through the year 2005.

The outlook for musical conductors is not especially positive. Competition is always fierce for the limited jobs that exist.

Musical Strategies

The Job Search

Getting ready for a job search is like getting ready to do battle; you must arm yourself with all the best weapons available to you and plan the best possible plan of attack. The best weapons available to you include a well-designed resume, a well-conceived cover letter, a well-selected portfolio, and an audition tape in the form of video or audio.

The Resume

A resume should include significant information that would make an employer want to hire you above all others. Standing as a summary of your experience, skills and abilities, strengths, accomplishments, and education, the resume's importance cannot be underestimated.

Experts agree that the best approach is to keep a resume focused and as brief as possible. Complete sentences are not necessary; phrases are acceptable. Keep to a maximum of two pages—one is even better. Don't list everything you ever did in your life; highlight important skills and accomplishments.

One type of resume, the chronological resume, includes the following elements:

Heading

Provide a heading at the top of the page that includes your name home address, E-mail, and phone number(s). (Invest in an answering machine or answering service if you don't already have one—an absolute necessity!)

Work Experience

This will be the main part of your resume, where your prospective employers will focus to determine whether or not you have the right qualifications for the job. So here is where you must show your expertise by emphasizing your accomplishments. Work experience is usually listed in reverse chronological order beginning with your most recent position. Entries should be complete, listing the job title, dates of employment, employer, and location, as well as descriptions of your responsibilities in each position. Use action verbs. Passive words don't have the same impact.

Education

Next to work experience, education is most important. Include all of the schools you've attended, the degrees you've earned, your field of concentration, and relevant extracurricular activities (student choral director, for example).

Other Elements

In addition, your resume might include the following sections:

Professional associations

Awards and honors

Special skills

References

The Cover Letter

A cover letter is a document that sells the recipient on reading the resume. It should be directed to a specific person whose name and spelling you have verified. Cover letters should be tailored to each specific company or job opening. Don't use a form letter here, although some of the information, including the job you are seeking and some elements of your professional background, may be the same.

Cover letters should consist of the following elements:

1. A salutation to the person who can hire you.

2. The opening, something that catches the attention of the reader. Be creative! Introduce yourself and specify the job for which you want to be considered. If you have a referral name, by all means mention it, and if you are responding to an ad, state that. If possible, show your researching skills by pointing out something new or positive you know about this employment possibility.

3. The body provides a brief summary of your qualifications for the job and refers to the resume, which will reinforce your selling campaign to win an interview or audition.

4. In the closing, request an interview and state your intention to follow up with a call, preferably on a specific date. Use the standard "Sincerely yours" and type your name leaving room for you to sign in between. It's not a bad idea to put your address and phone number under your name in the event the letter gets separated from the resume, which includes that information.

Avenues to Jobs

Those who study music at educational institutions may find their first jobs by going through their school placement offices.

Working closely with these human resource professionals can provide you with a wealth of worthwhile advice. For example, since orchestra musicians usually audition for positions after completing their formal training, school employment services may provide you with a list of possible locations.

Finding positions through want ads or ads published in trade journals is still a popular form of securing jobs. Also, professional organizations and associations may offer you direct employment possibilities or provide you with agencies, companies, or other employers or contacts that may eventually evolve into positions. Consider joining one that caters to your own musical specialty or to the field of music in general.

It is important to know that the truth is that, no matter what the field, the majority of people find their jobs through networking. That means that you must make a concerted effort to let people know what your expertise is and that you are available. Talk to friends and acquaintances; go to club meetings and association workshops. Volunteer to help with an event. Converse with people you deal with in everyday life: cleaners, bank tellers, personal accountants, anyone you can think of. Of course, you may not hear about an opening directly, but one person may give you the name of another to contact, which will eventually lead to a job. In the music business, it is wise to get to know as many people as possible, not only to make contacts that will lead to jobs, but in order to make contacts that may lead to internships, volunteer, or part-time work.

Send a resume and cover letter to everyone you know that has any link to the music business. Let people know if you have a videocassette or audiotape of you performing. If they want to hear it, they'll get back in touch. Don't send these things out if they are not requested. Keep track of the responses and follow up with people you don't hear from.

Individual musicians often join together with others to form local bands. Once formed, you can advertise by placing ads, putting up notices, and spreading the message by word of mouth.

After building a reputation, you may be able to obtain work through a booking agent or be qualified to become part of larger, more established groups.

After having some performing under your belt, you might visit recording studios and talk to anyone you can. Tell them about yourself, your experience, your musical specialties. Make sure you leave your business card (or a sheet with the information listed) with your instrument written on it. In fact, always carry cards with you and pass them out whenever you possibly can. You may need to have a demo tape made to leave with possible employers. Demos are recordings of your work, singing or instrumental, that display your talents at their very best.

For the Born Actors
(or Those Who Wish to Be Made Actors)

Actors and actresses are performers who play roles or parts in comedic, musical, or dramatic productions. This includes performances onstage, on television, in motion pictures, and on radio. In an attempt to both communicate and entertain, actors utilize speech, gestures, movement, and body language. In this way they operate as the principals who tell us a story.

The work of actors begins long before they perform in front of an audience or camera. Prior to the actual production, they analyze the theme of the play, study the script, scrutinize the character they are to play, memorize the lines, gain a concrete understanding of the director's viewpoint, become familiar with the cues that bring them on and off the stage, and often spend long, tedious hours in rehearsals.

In some ways, the media in which actors work (whether it is on the legitimate stage, in movies, or in television) determines to what extent they must prepare for their parts. For example, performers assigned roles in musical comedies played onstage may not only have to memorize speaking lines, but also to sing, dance, and carry out other functions in connection with their parts. (This may mean taking vocal or dancing instructions in order to fulfill the requirements of the role.) Their roles may require them to speak with appropriate accents or speech patterns associated with the characters or the locale of the production (such as in *West Side Story*) or to learn distinctive physical movements and gestures that are specific to the characters they are playing. In some cases, they may be required to apply appropriate makeup, although in many cases, makeup artists are employed to accomplish this.

Usually, actors and actresses who perform in stage shows rehearse for longer periods of time than do radio or television performers. Lines, actions, and cues must be perfect before the public sees the show. Musicals and stage plays may run for weeks or even years, although the people assuming the various roles may change. Rehearsals for a drama production may run about four weeks while musicals may take one or two additional weeks.

Radio performers are not required to practice as extensively as stage or film performers must since they can read their lines without having to memorize them. However, they must be sure to put a lot of feeling and emotion into their voices so that listeners may gain an understanding and appreciation for the characters without ever seeing them.

Weekly television shows and commercials are frequently filmed or taped in shorter periods of time. Miniseries or specials may call for longer periods of rehearsal time. Many of the television programs currently being scheduled are weekly series and all rehearsals and filming are accomplished in six days or less. Special shows or films made exclusively for television take much more preparation than weekly series shows. Since most television productions are prerecorded on film or video tape, the rehearsal and filming techniques are similar to those used by the movie industry.

Generally movie actors and actresses don't rehearse a movie from the beginning to the end. They work on small segments one at a time and the cameras roll to film these short scenes. Later, the film editors put the scenes in proper order.

Relatively few actors and actresses achieve star status in any of the mediums of stage, motion pictures, or television. A somewhat larger number are well-known, experienced performers who are frequently cast in supporting roles. Many successful actors continue to accept small roles, including commercials and product endorsements. Actors or actresses who accept nonspeaking parts are usually called day players or extras. Sometimes hundreds of extras are hired for movies—especially for scenes in which there are many people assembled together for a large scale event (like the Super Bowl, for instance). To become a movie extra, one must usually be listed by a casting agency, such as Central Casting, a no-fee agency that supplies all extras to the major movie studios in Hollywood. Applicants are accepted only when the number of persons of a particular type on the list—for example, athletic young women, old men, or small children—is below the foreseeable need.

Between engagements, actors refine and develop their talents by taking vocal, dancing, and acting lessons. They also may make personal appearances, accept offers to perform benefit shows, or teach drama courses to aspiring actors.

Who Is Looking for Actors?

Performers are hired for stage shows, for appearances in film, for commercials, and for parts on radio and television. New York and Hollywood are the most likely places to acquire employment. Next most likely would be Boston, Chicago, Seattle, Dallas, Miami, Minneapolis, and San Francisco. However, most larger cities have some kind of theatre groups. And even smaller towns usually have acting groups that offer a chance to gain some experience and employment. These would include little theatres, children's theatres, and regional and community theatres. Summer stock tours take actors and actresses all around the United States.

What's It Like to Be an Actor?

The life of an actor or actress is usually an uncertain one—individuals always face the anxiety of unsteady employment and the disappointment of rejections. And because there are often long periods of unemployment between jobs, acting demands patience and total commitment.

Performers must be available for constant rehearsals that may be stressful and physically and mentally exhausting—a situation exacerbated by script and/or cast changes. Performers often spend several weeks rehearsing their parts and some rehearsals may be scheduled on weekends, holidays, and evenings. Those having small roles may wait for hours before being called to rehearse their parts.

Rehearsals may take place amid the clutter of electricians, camera operators, painters, carpenters, and stagehands. Heavy costumes and hot lights may be necessary. Deadlines loom in this business, too, and performers may be called upon to accomplish quite a bit in a very short period of time. In fact, a performer may rehearse one production in the morning and afternoon and perform another every evening.

The type of role being played often determines the amount of physical exertion required. For some roles, performers move about a great deal when walking or running, riding horses, dancing, or performing hazardous stunts. (A professionally trained "stunt person" usually undertakes the more dangerous stunts.)

Considerable traveling is often required of performers employed by theatrical road companies. These individuals perform the same play in a series of different locations. They frequently give an evening performance in one city and spend the following day traveling to the theatre where their next performance is to be given. They must adjust to the varying facilities and equipment available in each theatre. Movie personnel are also required to travel to sites that have been chosen as film locations.

The physical surroundings of actors performing in stage productions can range from modern, air-conditioned, comfortable, and well-equipped theatres to those which are old and have inadequate facilities. Backstage areas of many theatres are crowded, dusty, drafty, and poorly ventilated. Actors may be provided private dressing rooms or apply their makeup and change costumes in areas shared by several other performers.

The Road to Acting

Aspiring actors should take part in high school and college plays, and work with little theatres, summer stock, regional theatre, dinner theatre, children's theatre, and other acting groups for experience. (In fact, any stage work is useful.) Formal dramatic training or acting experience is generally necessary and is definitely advantageous, although some people do enter the field without it. Most people take college courses in theatre, arts, drama, and dramatic literature. Many experienced actors get additional formal training to learn new skills and improve old ones. Training can be obtained at dramatic arts schools in New York and Los Angeles, and at colleges and universities throughout the country offering bachelor's or higher degrees in dramatic and theatre arts.

College drama curriculums usually include courses in liberal arts, stage speech and movement, directing, playwriting, play production, design, and history of drama, as well as practical courses in acting. Other important areas include literature, dramatic arts, music, dance, communications, and English.

The curriculum catalog offered by the University of Illinois at Urbana-Champaign offers insights for prospective theatre majors:

"The curricular options in the Department of Theatre provide intensive and extensive preparation for the rigorous demands of a professional career in the theatre. A strong commitment to work in the theatre and a realistic understanding of its intellectual, aesthetic, and physical demands is therefore necessary in students who enter the department."

Before acceptance in the undergraduate programs in theatre at the University of Illinois, applicants must participate in one of several pre-admission workshops, which take place at the Krannert Center for the Performing Arts five or more weekends each year, and at selected regional locations (normally New York, Chicago, San Francisco, and Los Angeles). In these workshops, applicants who ultimately plan to pursue the curriculum in acting in their junior year should present a four-minute audition composed of two contrasting works from dramatic literature. Applicants who intend to pursue the performance studies curriculum should bring a portfolio of their previous theatre work, an original two-page script written specifically for the workshop, and any other written work that reflects the student's interests and accomplishments. Information on these workshops will be sent to applicants once their admissibility to the University has been determined by the Office of Admissions and Records.

Three curricula are offered in theatre: the Professional Studio in Acting; the Performance Studies Curriculum; and the Division of Design Technology and Management, which has specialized options in scene design, costume design and construction, theatre technology and lighting, and stage management. Students are formally admitted to these curricula only after an evaluation by the faculty during the student's second year. The programs in acting and theatre design, technology, and management are intended for students who, in the judgment of the faculty, are ready to con-

centrate in these specialties in an intensive undergraduate professional training curriculum.

The Department of Theatre sponsors the Illinois Repertory
Theatre, which is one of the resident producing organizations of
the Krannert Center for the Performing Arts. Illinois Repertory
Theatre produces eight fully mounted productions each academic
year and three each summer. The theatres and workshops of the
Krannert Center serve as laboratories for theatre students, who
have the opportunity to learn and to work alongside an outstanding staff of resident theatre professionals and visiting artists,
preparing performances in theatre, opera, and dance. In addition,
the department sponsors a small experimental theatre space for
student-directed productions.

Once you have your degree and some basic experience, the best
way to get started is to make use of opportunities close to you and
to build upon them. For example, regional theatre experience may
help in obtaining work in New York or Los Angeles. Modeling
experience may also be helpful.

Actors and actresses must have a sincere interest and affection
for acting, talent, training, poise, stage presence, the ability to
move an audience, the ability to follow directions, an appealing
physical appearance, and experience in order to succeed. Other
important qualities include hard work, self-confidence, dedication,
versatility, ambition, good health, patience, commitment, stamina,
the ability to memorize, the ability to withstand adverse conditions, perseverance, drive, determination, desire, discipline, and
the ability to handle emotional tension and disappointment.
Those who are self-conscious or withdrawn will not make it.

The length of a performer's working life depends largely on
training, skills, versatility, and perseverance. Some actors continue working throughout their lives; however, many leave the occupation after a short time because they cannot find enough work to
make a living.

Compensation for Actors

Minimum salaries, hours of work, and other conditions of employment are covered in collective bargaining agreements between producers of shows and unions representing workers in this field. The Actors' Equity Association (AEA) represents stage actors; the Screen Actors Guild (SAG) and the Screen Extras Guild (SEG) cover actors in motion pictures, including prime-time television, commercials, and films; and the American Federation of Television and Radio Artists (AFTRA) represents daytime television, recording, and radio performers.

Of course, any actor or director may negotiate for a salary higher than the minimum. Some well-known actors have salary rates well above the minimums, and the salaries of the few top stars are many times the figures cited, creating a false impression that all actors are highly paid.

Each motion picture is a separate entity and the terms may vary from one film to another. Some top stars receive a percentage of the box office sales along with their stated salary. Once agreed upon, contracts are drawn up which specify overtime and residual rights. (Residual rights are those payments made to actors or actresses for reruns of films, television shows and commercials.) Sometimes performers may receive residuals for pay television, cable television, or videotape sales.

According to limited information, the *Occupational Outlook Handbook* reports that the minimum weekly salary for actors in Broadway stage productions was $1,000 in 1995. Those in small off-Broadway theatres received minimums ranging from $380 to $650 a week, depending on the seating capacity of the theatre. For shows on the road, actors received about $100 more per day for living expenses. According to the Screen Actors Guild, motion picture and television actors with speaking parts earned, in 1995, a minimum daily rate of about $500 or $1750 for a five-day week. Those without speaking parts, extras, earned a minimum daily rate of about $100. Actors also receive contributions to their health and pension plans and additional compensation for reruns.

Earnings from acting are low because employment is so irregular. However, actors and actresses do work steady hours when they have a role in a play. Usually this translates to two matinees and six evening performances—a week of work is considered eight stage showings. More than this may translate to overtime pay. A basic work week after a show opens is thirty-six hours.

Many actors who work more than a set number of weeks per year are covered by a union health, welfare, and pension fund, including hospitalization insurance, to which employers contribute. Under some employment conditions, Actors' Equity and AFTRA members have paid vacations and sick leave.

How Does the Future Look for Actors?

Employment of actors is expected to grow faster than the average for all occupations through the year 2005. Rising foreign demand for American productions, combined with a growing domestic market—fueled by the growth of cable television, home movie rentals, and television syndications—should stimulate demand for actors and other production personnel. Growth of opportunities in recorded media should be accompanied by increasing jobs in live productions. Growing numbers of people who enjoy live theatrical entertainment will continue to go to theatres. Touring productions of Broadway plays and other large shows are providing new opportunities for actors and directors. However, employment may be somewhat affected by government funding for the arts—a decline in funding could dampen future employment growth in this segment of the entertainment industry. Workers leaving the field will continue to create more job openings than will growth.

The large number of people desiring acting careers and the lack of formal entry requirements should continue to cause keen competition for actor positions. Only the most talented will find regular employment.

Acting Strategies—Finding a Job

Armed with your college degree, basic knowledge of the acting business, and some experience, you'll need to prepare a portfolio that will highlight your qualifications, acting history, and special skills This will take the form of a resume. You will also need to have photos taken by a professional photographer, one who shows you off to your best advantage. These are the essential tools of your trade. Attach your resume to the back of your picture with one staple at the upper left- and right-hand corner. Once you have your portfolio ready, you can start making the rounds at casting offices, ad agencies, and producers' and agents' offices. Several trade newspapers contain casting information, ads for part-time jobs, information about shows, and other pertinent data about what's going on in the industry. Among these are *Back Stage* in New York and Los Angeles, *Ross Reports* in New York, and the weekly *Variety*. In Los Angeles, there's also *Daily Variety*, the *Hollywood Reporter*, and *Drama-Logue*.

Once you drop off your resumes and head shots, you shouldn't just sit at home waiting for the phone to ring. It's wise to stay in contact—stop by and say hello. Check in by phone every week to see if any opportunities are available for you. If you are currently in a show, send prospective employers a flyer. It shows them that you are a working actor.

When you get past this initial stage and actually win an audition, there are some things you should remember.

Audition Tips

1. Be prepared.

2. Be familiar with the piece—read it beforehand and choose the parts you'd like to try out for.

3. Go for it—don't hold back.

4. Speak loudly and clearly—project to the back of the room.

5. Take chances.

6. Try not to be the one going first—if you can observe others you can see what they do, correct their mistakes, and get a feel for the script.

7. Be enthusiastic and confident.

8. Keep auditioning—even if you don't get any parts, you are getting invaluable experience that is bound to pay off.

So when do you get an agent? Not right away, anyway. First of all, you don't need an agent to audition for everything. There are many things you can audition for that do not require an agent— theatre, nonunion films, union films. However, most commercials are cast through agencies, so you would most likely need an agent to land one of those.

While waiting to be chosen for a part, acting hopefuls often take jobs as waitresses, bartenders, or taxi drivers, for example— workers who are afforded a flexible schedule and money to live on.

Words from the Pros

Introducing—Jennifer Aquino

Jennifer Aquino grew up in Cerritos, California. She got her first taste of acting at St. Linus elementary school in Norwalk where she played the leading role of the princess in *Beyond the Horizon*. Continuing with success in this area, she received the Performing Arts Award while attending Whitney High School. Subsequently, she graduated from the University of California (Los Angeles), where she studied theatre and dance and received a bachelor of arts degree in economics. (After all, the entertainment industry is a business!) As a member of the dance team, she was a UCLA cheerleader for three years. In addition to cheering for UCLA's football and basketball teams, she also entered national dance team competitions.

Following her college graduation, she got her first break playing Eolani, the wife of Dr. Jacoby in David Lynch's television series *Twin Peaks* (a result of her very first audition). Then she got an agent and joined the Screen Actors Guild. She has been performing in various theatrical productions and is a founding member of Theatre Geo, as well as an active member of Theatre West and the East West Players Network. (Watch for her in a national commercial for Ford trucks.)

Jennifer's television credits include: *Weird Science; The Paranormal Borderline; Fresh Prince of Bel Air; Santa Barbara;* and *Twin Peaks.* Her film credits include *The Party Crashers; Prisoners of Love;* AFI's *it makes you wonder . . . how a girl can keep from going under;* UCLA's *Fleeting Vanities of Life;* USC's *Unexpected Love;* and NYU's *Free Love.* Theatre credits include *People Like Me* at the Playwrights' Arena; *Gila River* at Japan America Theatre and at Scottsdale Center for the Arts in Arizona; *Cabaret* and *Sophisticated Barflies* at East West Players; PAWS/LA Gala Benefit at the Pasadena Playhouse; S.T.A.G.E. Benefit at the Luckman Theatre; *The Really Early Dinner Theatre for Kids* at The Hollywood Playhouse; *Boys' Life, Hold Me!, Scruples,* and *Watermelon Boats* at Theatre West; *Mistletoe Mews* at Theatre Geo; and *Is Nudity Required?* at Playhouse of the Foothills.

"I remember performing at family gatherings ever since I was a little kid," says Jennifer. "I always enjoyed being in the spotlight. To me, acting is like a child's game of pretend, something I always enjoyed. I see it as a career where you can earn a lot of money while having a lot of fun. At the same time you are entertaining people, impacting them, making them think, making them feel certain emotions, educating them, and helping them escape from their current lives.

"Most actors who are starting out hold some kind of side job, day job, or part-time job," she continues. "For me, it was a career in the health-care industry working for Kaiser Foundation Health Plan. I then became a health care consultant for one of the Big Six accounting firms, Deloitte & Touche. I was such a good employee that my managers would be flexible and let me go out on auditions. After a few years, I realized that I was working too many hours (seventy to eighty per week), and I finally had to make a decision to quit my day job and focus 100 percent of my time toward acting. After booking a few jobs, including a national commercial, I was able to do so. It was a big risk, but one I felt necessary to take. I remember what my acting coach would say— 'Part-time work gets part-time results.' The more I put into acting, the more I got out of it.

"Don't be fooled, though—acting is a lot of hard work. I am at it seven days a week, mornings, afternoons, evenings, weekends (forty to sixty hours per week). And if I'm not working on the creative side of acting (which is doing my homework for a job that I booked or for an audition) I'm working on the business side of acting—talking to my agents, managers, networking, sending my head shots to casting directors, producers, directors, writers, attending seminars, meeting people, etc. I also try to keep my stress level down, and take care of myself by getting enough sleep, exercising, eating healthy, and having some relaxation time. And I have been fortunate—the sets I've worked on have all been positive experiences for me.

"What I like most about my work is that I can say that I am making a living doing what I absolutely love to do, and that I am pursuing my passion in life. Not too many people in this world can say that. What I like least about my work is that there are a lot of politics in it. It's not always the best actor who gets the job. Some of the time, it's a certain look, what your credits are, who you know, etc., that determines who gets the job. There are a lot of things that are out of your control. That's just part of the business and you have to accept it.

"I would advise anyone who is considering acting as a career to pursue your dreams and be persistent—but only if it's something you absolutely love to do, and there's nothing else in the world you would rather do. Pursue the creative as well as the business side of acting. Don't let anyone stop you from doing what you want to do. And always keep up your craft by continuing your training."

Introducing Gonzo Schexnayder

Gonzo Schexnayder earned a bachelor's degree in journalism and advertising at Louisiana State University in Baton Rouge, Louisiana. He attended various acting classes at LSU and Monterey Peninsula College in Monterey, California. He also attended Chicago's Second City Training Center for over a year and the Actors Center following that. He is a SAG and AFTRA member.

"I had always wanted to do stand-up comedy but didn't pursue it until graduating from college, when I began working with an improvisational comedy group," he says. "Four months later, the military sent me to Monterey, California, for language training. While there, I did my first staged reading and my first show. I'd never felt such elation as when I performed. Nothing in my life had given me the sheer thrill and rush that I experienced by creating a character and maintaining that throughout a given period of time. Nothing else mattered but that moment on stage, my other actors, and the scene we were performing.

"After completing the language program in November of 1990, I returned to Baton Rouge. There I began the long process of introspection about my career choices and what I wanted to do. I began to audition locally and started reading and studying acting. I still had not made the jump to being an actor, I was merely investigating the possibility.

"One night while watching an interview with John Goodman, I realized how important acting had become to me. I knew that it possibly meant a life of macaroni and cheese and Ramen noodles, but I knew that up until that moment, nothing had made me as happy or as motivated. While I believe I had the skills and the drive to make it in advertising (or whatever career I chose), I decided that acting was my only logical choice.

"Whether it's rehearsing a show, performing improvisation in front of an audience, or even auditioning for a commercial, it's fun. If you can separate the sense of rejection most actors feel from not getting a part, auditioning for anything becomes your job. Rehearsing becomes your life. Just as a carpenter's job is building a house, as an actor, I look at my job as building my performance. The final product is there for me to look at and admire (if executed well), but the path to that product is the thrill.

"Unfortunately, I'm not at a point in my career where I'm making enough money to quit my day job. I'm close, but not close enough. I still feel the need to have some sense of financial stability or I lapse into thinking about money. It's all about balance and deciding what's really important. Sure I'd love to have an apartment with central air and a balcony. I'd love to have a car that is still under warranty. But I know that by putting my efforts and money into my acting career, those other things don't matter. What matters is how it makes me feel. Cars and apartments don't give me the satisfaction that being an actor does.

"How many hours and how busy I am depends on what I'm doing. Over the last year I've worked with five other actors to open our own theatre, Broad Shoulders Theatre, and have found my time constrained. On top of that I have been pursuing (with some success) a voice-over/on-camera career in addition to working a full-time job. Yesterday I finished six days of shooting on a graduate thesis film and last weekend we opened our first show (TheatreSports/Chicago, Improvisational Comedy) at our new theatre. We have another opening (which I'm not performing in) tonight and expect to open four more shows in the next three months. I've also taken a year of guitar classes and maintained my presence in acting and on-camera classes and workshops. I'm always busy and continually looking for the next chance to market myself and increase my salability as an actor.

"I love the process of acting and sometimes just the fast-paced, eclectic nature of the business. There is always something new to learn and something new to try. The sheer excitement of performing live is amazing and the personal satisfaction of getting an audience to laugh or cry simply by your words and actions is very gratifying.

"I dislike pretentious actors and people who take advantage of an actor's desire to perform. As one of the only professions where there is an abundance of people willing to work for nothing, producers, casting directors, agents, and managers who only care about the money will take advantage of and abuse actors for personal gain. Being an astute actor helps prevent much of this, but one must always be on the lookout.

"I would advise others who are interested in this career to work where you are. Perfect your craft. Move when you have to—you will know when it's time. And above all—trust your instincts."

> Here's another birth name challenge:
> Allen Stewart Konisberg

For More Information

Periodicals for Performers

Back Stage. 1515 Broadway, New York, NY 10036.

Back Stage West. 5055 Wilshire Boulevard, Los Angeles, CA 90036.

Billboard. 1515 Broadway, New York, NY 10036.

Cash Box. 51 East Eighth Street, Suite 155, New York, NY 10003.

Daily Variety. 5700 Wilshire Boulevard, Suite 120, Los Angeles, CA 90036.

Musician. 1515 Broadway, New York, NY 10036.
Variety. Cahners Publishing, 475 Park Avenue South, New York, NY 10016.

Organizations for Musicians

There are literally hundreds of professional associations that provide benefits to members.

Academy of Country Music (ACM)
500 Sunnyside Boulevard
Woodbury, NY 11797

American Choral Directors Association (ACDA)
P. O. Box 6310
Lawton, OK 73506

American Federation of Musicians (AFM)
1501 Broadway, Suite 600
New York, NY 10036

American Federation of Television and Radio Artists (AFTRA)
260 Madison Avenue
New York, NY 10016

American Guild of Music (AGM)
5354 Washington Street, Box 3
Downers Grove, IL 60515

American Guild of Musical Artists (AGMA)
1727 Broadway
New York, NY 10019

American Guild of Organists (AGO)
475 Riverside Drive, Suite 1260
New York, NY 10115

American Music Conference (AMC)
5140 Avenida Encinas
Carlsbad, CA 92008

American Musicological Society (AMS)
201 South 34th Street
University of Pennsylvania
Philadelphia, PA 19104

American Symphony Orchestra League (ASOL)
777 Fourteenth Street NW, Suite 500
Washington, DC 20005

Association of Canadian Orchestras
56 The Esplanade, Suite 311
Toronto, Ontario M5EIA7
Canada

Black Music Association (BMA)
1775 Broadway
New York, NY 10019

Broadcast Music, Inc. (BMI)
320 West 57th Street
New York, NY 10019

Chamber Music America
545 Eighth Avenue
New York, NY 10018

Chorus America
Association of Professional Vocal Ensembles
2111 Sansom Street
Philadelphia, PA 19103

College Music Society
202 West Spruce
Missoula, MT 59802

Concert Artists Guild (CAG)
850 Seventh Avenue, Room 1003
New York, NY 10019

Country Music Association (CMA)
P. O. Box 22299
One Music Circle South
Nashville, TN 37203

Gospel Music Association (GMA)
P. O. Box 23201
Nashville, TN 37202

International Conference of Symphony and Opera Musicians
    (ICSOM)
6607 Waterman
St. Louis, MO 63130

Metropolitan Opera Association (MOA)
Lincoln Center
New York NY 10023

National Academy of Popular Music (NAPM)
885 Second Avenue
New York, NY 10017

National Academy of Recording Arts and Sciences (NARAS)
303 North Glen Oaks Boulevard, Suite 140
Burbank, CA 91502

National Association of Music Theaters
John F. Kennedy Center
Washington, DC 20566

National Association of Schools of Music
11250 Roger Bacon Drive, Suite 21
Reston, VA 22091

National Orchestral Association (NOA)
474 Riverside Drive, Room 455
New York, NY 10115

National Symphony Orchestra Association (NSOA)
JFK Center For The Performing Arts
Washington, DC 20566

Opera America
777 Fourteenth Street NW, Suite 520
Washington, DC 20005

Society of Professional Audio Recording Studios
4300 Tenth Avenue North, Number 2
Lake Worth, FL 33461

Touring Entertainment Industry Association (TEIA)
1203 Lake Street
Fort Worth, TX 76102

Women in Music
P. O. Box 441
Radio City Station
New York, NY 10010

Organizations for Actors

Actors Equity Association
165 West 46th Street
New York, NY 10036

Alliance of Canadian Cinema
Television and Radio Artists
2239 Yonge Street
Toronto, Ontario M5S2B5
Canada

Alliance of Resident Theaters/New York
325 Spring Street
New York, NY 10013

American Alliance for Theater and Education
P. O. Box 87341
Department of Theater
Arizona State University
Tempe, AZ 85287

American Federation of Television and Radio Artists (AFTRA)
260 Madison Avenue
New York, NY 10016

American Film Institute
P. O. Box 27999
2021 North Western Avenue
Los Angeles, CA 90027

American Guild of Variety Artists (AVA)
184 Fifth Avenue
New York, NY 10019

American Theater Association (ATA)
1010 Wisconsin Avenue NW
Washington, DC 20007

American Theatre Works, Inc.
Theatre Directories
P. O. Box 519
Dorset, VT 05251

Canadian Actors Equity Association
260 Richmond Street East
Toronto, Ontario M5A1P4
Canada

National Arts Jobbank
141 East Palace Avenue
Santa Fe, NM 87501

National Association of Schools of Theatre
11250 Roger Bacon Drive, Suite 21
Reston, VA 22090

Screen Actors Guild (SAG)
1515 Broadway
New York, NY 10036

Screen Actors Guild (SAG)
7065 Hollywood Boulevard
Hollywood, CA 90028

Theater Communications Group, Inc.
355 Lexington Avenue
New York, NY 10017

Name Quiz Answers

Chapter One—Jerome Silberman is Gene Wilder

Chapter Two—Joseph Levitch is Jerry Lewis

Chapter Three—Joan Alexandra Molinsky is Joan Rivers

Chapter Four—Melvin Kaminsky is Mel Brooks

Chapter Five—Nathan Birnbaum is George Burns

Chapter Six—Allen Stewart Konisberg is Woody Allen

About the Author

J an Goldberg's love for the printed page began well before her second birthday. Regular visits to the book bindery where her grandfather worked produced a magic combination of sights and smells that she carries with her to this day.

Childhood was filled with composing poems and stories, reading books, and playing library. Elementary and high school included an assortment of contributions to school newspapers. While a full-time college student, Goldberg wrote extensively as part of her job responsibilities in the College of Business Administration at Roosevelt University in Chicago. After receiving a degree in elementary education, she was able to extend her love of reading and writing to her students.

Goldberg has written extensively in the occupations area for General Learning Corporation's *Career World Magazine*, as well as for the many career publications produced by CASS Communications. She has also contributed to a number of projects for educational publishers, including Scott Foresman, Addison-Wesley, and Camp Fire Boys and Girls.

As a feature writer, Goldberg's work has appeared in *Parenting Magazine*, *Today's Chicago Woman*, *Opportunity Magazine*, *Chicago Parent*, *Correspondent*, *Opportunity Magazine*, *Successful Student*, *Complete Woman*, *North Shore Magazine*, and the Pioneer Press newspapers. In all, she has published more than 250 pieces as a full-time freelance writer.

In addition to *Careers for Class Clowns*, she is the author of *On the Job: Real People Working in Communications*, *On the Job: Real*

People Working in Entertainment, Great Jobs for Music Majors, Great Jobs for Computer Science Majors, Careers for Courageous People, Careers in Journalism, Great Jobs for Accounting Majors, On the Job: Real People Working in Science, Opportunities in Research and Development Careers, and *Opportunities in Horticulture Careers,* all published by NTC/Contemporary Publishing Group.